Mankind Discovering

Volume I
A plan for new galleries at the Royal Ontario Museum

Prepared by
the Exhibits Communication Task Force
with the assistance of
Urban Design Consultants

RŌM

Royal Ontario Museum
1978

Editorial Committee

J. Di Profio
M. Allodi
A. G. Edmund
N. B. Millet

Foreword

With the publication of *Mankind Discovering: A Plan for New Galleries at the Royal Ontario Museum* the work of the Exhibits Communication Task Force is completed. As the culmination of twenty-two months of activities, this document represents a very large commitment by the members of the ECTF and by the staff of the Museum. *Mankind Discovering* provides a plan for the development of the Royal Ontario Museum's galleries over the next twenty years. We believe it is a unique account of the processes and procedures of gallery development at a major museum in Canada, and to the best of our knowledge, in North America.

This accomplishment was possible only because the ECTF members devoted a great deal of time, energy, and enthusiasm to the tasks assigned to them by the Director in September 1976. As their Chairman, I would like to thank them for their dedication, steadfastness, constant good humour, and goodwill. The Task Force members were:

M. Allodi, Canadiana Department

P. Buerschaper, Exhibit Design Services Department

G. Edmund, Vertebrate Palaeontology Department (as of February, 1977)

J. Hillen, Exhibit Design Services Department

L. Levine, West Asian Department (Vice-chairman)

R. Madeley, Education Services Department (as of July, 1977)

R. Moynes, Education Services Department (to May, 1977)

R. Peterson, Mammalogy Department (to April, 1978)

E. Phillimore, Conservation Department

H. Sears, Urban Design Consultants (Coordinator)

H. Shih, Far Eastern Department (to December, 1976)

Various working groups helped the ECTF to define, plan, and carry out specific projects, particularly during the first phase of activity. Their efforts significantly eased the work load of the ECTF and were greatly appreciated.

The ECTF and the Museum community are especially grateful to the Director, Dr. James E. Cruise, for establishing an essential participatory process and for carefully considering the recommendations of the ECTF within the overall needs of the Museum. His advice and direction throughout the process were invaluable.

The staff of the Royal Ontario Museum also deserves our gratitude for its participation in the development of this document. Although the procedures were time-consuming and occasionally stressful they resulted in an approach to communicating with the visitor which would otherwise have been impossible.

To the firm of Urban Design Consultants, and in particular to Henry Sears, all members of the ECTF extend a special vote of thanks. Mr. Sears oversaw the scheduling and coordinated the activities of the ECTF. His energy and enthusiasm were major contributions that affected every ECTF member. UDC staff members Betty Kaser and Gail Burgess must also be thanked for their work in drafting innumerable reports for the ECTF.

We also express our appreciation to Jan Schroer, Assistant Coordinator, who provided support for the ECTF and its working groups throughout the project.

We hope that the efforts of all these people will find glorious fulfilment in our expanded and renovated Museum. We believe that this report will provide an effective master plan for the development of the galleries in the future ROM. We leave its implementation to our successors.

Joseph R. Di Profio
Chairman, ECTF

August, 1978

Contents

PART III
THE PLAN

PART IV

IMPLEMENTING THE PLAN

APPENDICES

List of Figures and Tables in the Text

FIGURES

TABLES

List of Figures and Tables in the Appendix

Introduction

Introduction

The Royal Ontario Musuem (ROM) is an institution of great scope and complexity. It comprises more than twenty curatorial departments both of art and archaeology and of the sciences. The present allocation of gallery space among the various departments and the arrangement of galleries withing the existing H-shaped building reflect the *ad hoc* nature of the ROM's development since 1914. Floor plans of both the existing and the expanded buildings are included as Appendix A of this report.

Planning for the renovation and expansion of galleries has demanded meticulous consideration of the needs both of the institution as a whole and of its extensive collections, its visitors, its individual departments, and its staff.

The role of the Exhibits Communication Task Force (ECTF) in planning for the renovated and expanded Museum was described in Director's Memorandum No. 42, dated September 15, 1976:

> An Exhibits Communication Task Force is being established to carry on the second phase of the work begun by the Communications Design Team. The CDT has produced a report entitled *Communicating with the Museum Visitor* which deals with underlying principles and best approaches to the development of museum exhibits so that they may communicate most effectively with their audiences. It will be the job of the Exhibits Communication Task Force to apply the ideas from the CDT report in the development of policies and plans for communication and education through the galleries and exhibits of the Royal Ontario Museum...

The specific objective for the ECTF is to prepare for my approval the following:

(1)   a list of new galleries or exhibits, representing new types or new subject areas, that should be added to those presently extant at the ROM;

(2)   a master plan for the placement of all galleries and exhibits within the present and planned ROM buildings;

(3)   a set of priorities for the replacement or renovation of extant galleries and exhibits and for the construction of entirely new ones required by the expansion;

(4)   recommendations on the allocation of $3,000,000* in expansion funds to the creation of new galleries and exhibits and the replacement of those affected by these plans and the ROM expansion;

(5)   a theme (and/or sub-themes) for the exhibits and galleries of the ROM and how it might best be communicated through them;

(6)   a set of operational policies on gallery and exhibit communication with visitors to the ROM.

The efforts of the ECTF to fulfil these objectives have taken place within a comprehensive planning programme. Under the coordination of the Project Office, Planning Group 1, made up of the architects and sub-consultants, has been responsible for planning new buildings and mechanical renovations to the present spaces; Group 2, the ECTF, has been responsible for planning exhibits and galleries; and Group 3 for capital funds acquisition.

In November 1977, a major phase of the overall planning process for the ROM ended with the completion of the *Final Planning Report* by the Project Office. This report provided a full description of the new and renovated facilities proposed for the Museum within the budget limits set by the Board of Trustees, and a discussion of related matters.

---

*This amount was increased to $4,000,000 in November, 1976 by the Board of Trustees.

As noted in the *Final Planning Report,* the ECTF was continuing
to plan the allocation and arrangement of the approximately
215,000 square feet of new and renovated gallery space and
was to report separately on its proposals. With the completion of this report, *Mankind Discovering* , containing the overall gallery plan for the renovated and expanded Museum, the
ECTF has fulfilled that task. The work of planning galleries,
however, is far from over. This report provides the framework for gallery development. The task of overseeing that
development will fall to the committee established to succeed
the ECTF.

The work of the ECTF began in September 1976 and has taken
place in two main stages. The first stage consisted of a
number of short-term measures designed to deal with various
matters requiring immediate attention. These were described
in the report *Opportunities and Constraints,* released on June 1,
1977.

The physical changes made in the Museum as a result of the
first stage were as follows:

- a new student entrance was completed, in
  conjunction with renovations to the theatre
  to make it more attractive and to accommodate maintenance and storage facilities;

- renovations were made in the Rotunda, including
  the installation of a central information and
  reception desk, and the mounting of a directory
  as the first step in developing a consistent
  orientation system;

- an experimental Discovery Room was opened in
  July 1977;

- a display case was installed for temporary
  exhibits on the Museum's research activities;

- a variety of gallery improvements were undertaken,
  including the construction of a new Arthropod
  Gallery and an Introductory Life Sciences gallery
  designed to explore the use of interdisciplinary
  concepts.

All of these projects were experimental prototypes for the
main renovation and expansion programme.

The main purpose of the *Opportunities and Constraints* report was, however, to recommend principles and procedures for developing an overall gallery plan for the ROM. Among other things, the report:

- explored the potential of the Museum's collections, as presented by the curatorial departments, as a means of communicating with the public;

- discussed the constraints imposed on planning by limitations of space, funds, and staff;

- recommended principles for resolving problems concerning individual galleries (particularly the allocation of gallery space), departmental, interdisciplinary, and general galleries (see Appendix B, Bulletin #6), and effective communication with visitors to the galleries;

- emphasized the need to develop a plan for dealing with such Museum-wide concerns as the Museum's image, a ROM theme (a specific theme was recommended), visitor orientation and circulation, and the conservation, maintenance, and security of the collections;

- made detailed recommendations for the process to be followed in the next stage of its work - the development of an overall gallery plan.

Opportunities and Constraints was circulated to all the Museum staff for comments in June 1977, and was then revised and submitted to the Director. Upon receipt of the Director's approval in August 1977, the ECTF began the second stage of its activities: the construction of a plan for applying the principles presented in that report. This plan constitutes the main part of *Mankind Discovering*.

Part I
The Work of the Exhibits Communication Task Force

Part I
The Work of the Exhibits
Communication Task Force

The work of the ECTF was notable for two things in particular. First, there was continual consultation with the Museum
staff throughout. Such consultation was facilitated by the
fact that all the committee members except the coordinator
held full-time positions in the Museum.

Another means of communication was provided by bulletins
distributed by the ECTF to all staff members at a number of
crucial points. The purposes of these bulletins were (a) to
keep the staff informed about the progress of the committee's
work; (b) to solicit the views and opinions of the staff;
and (c) to make it known that ECTF members were always
available for discussion and questioning. Some of the bulletins
distributed are reproduced in Appendix B.

The second notable thing was the amount of time and energy
expended by the committee members in order to finish their job
in the limited time available.

One of the commitments undertaken by ECTF members was to
attend regular meetings for the discussion of all matters
within their terms of reference. During the twenty-two months
of the committee's operation, the members attended at least
two full ECTF meetings a month, and as many as seven a month
in the busier periods. The matters discussed included requests
for gallery renovations, gallery proposals from individual
departments or staff members, the result of various ECTF
investigations, and all information useful in overseeing the
work of its sub-groups.

The most demanding part of the whole process, however, was
the series of interviews that constituted the main method
of consultation with the separate Museum departments. The

preparation for these interviews was as time-consuming as the interviews themselves. In the first stage of the work ECTF members interviewed all curatorial departments and many non-curatorial departments to gather their views and concerns about galleries. In the second stage, when more specific and detailed information and opinions were required, two series of interviews were held with the departments or with groups of departments.

To cut down the number of full ECTF meetings, sub-groups were assigned responsibility for specific departments or groups of departments. Only the ECTF coordinator attended all meetings and was a member of every team. Each sub-group conducted the interviews with its assigned departments, considered the information obtained, developed ideas arising out of the discussions, and presented its findings to the task force. In this way all members had the opportunity to gain a wide knowledge of the gallery-related requirements and concerns of individual departments and of the Museum as a whole.

Members of the ECTF visited a number of other North American museums to interview their staffs. These visits had two purposes: first, to record the experience of other museums in planning and developing galleries and to learn what had been found to work and what had not; and secondly, to gain a wider knowledge of the ways in which exhibits can be used for communication, as a foundation for new departures.

The twenty-two institutions visited included art museums, science museums, and museums that, like the ROM, are both in one. The interviews were particularly intensive at museums that had recently undergone expansion or renovation. Each ECTF member visited at least one other museum, and most visited several. A list of the museums visited will be found in Appendix C.

Another responsibility of the ECTF was to arrange for a programme of survey and evaluation activities as the most effective way of finding out in what ways the present galleries do or do not achieve their purpose, and how visitors use the Museum.

Conservation was immediately identified as one topic requiring intensive study. A micro-climate workshop was organized to find, with the help of outside specialists practical methods of providing micro-climates at the ROM.

The information gathered by the ECTF was organized into an archive for future reference. It includes:

- the interviews with the curatorial departments of the ROM;

- the gallery proposals received;

- accounts of the visits and interviews conducted at other musuems and the photographic records obtained;

- the results of the survey and evaluation activities;

- the report on the micro-climate workshop.

In addition, there is a record of each stage of the process by which the overall gallery plan was developed, including all the discussions of the ECTF and its working groups. Together, all these records constitute an extensive and valuable collection of information for those who will be responsible for the detailed stages of gallery planning and construction.

The accomplishments of the ECTF have owed a great deal to the committee's structure. Because the heavy work load imposed on each member had to be borne along with his or her other Museum duties, the ECTF could not have operated successfully without additional support. A staff was made available for this purpose by the ECTF coordinator (an outside consultant). This staff was responsible for developing the planning processes for the ECTF, for monitoring the progress of its work, for undertaking investigations, for arranging interviews with departments, and for formulating plans and communication objectives for the galleries. The division of responsibilities, with the consultant's staff doing the day-to-day work under the direction of the ECTF, proved to be a successful method for getting the job done.

Part II
Developing the Plan

Part II
Developing the Plan

A. Departmental Contributions to the Plan:
Descriptions and Findings

The contributions of individual Museum departments to the ECTF's work have occasionally seemed an overwhelming burden to both groups and participants. Nevertheless, the resulting exchange of ideas, opinions, and suggestions has been necessary to the development of the overall gallery plan. This development has been essentially a process of discovering the objectives and requirements of the curatorial departments regarding galleries and, as far as possible, realizing them in a rational and comprehensible plan.

1. INITIAL INTERVIEWS WITH DEPARTMENTS

The ECTF began by holding discussions about the galleries with all the curatorial departments and with several non-curatorial departments. The ideas that emerged from these interviews showed the direction the detailed planning should take. It was generally felt that:

- Departmental galleries were essential to the integrity of the collections.

- Interdisciplinary concepts such as ecology and evolution should be presented.

- Departments were interested in communicating with the public about their research and functions.

- There were inefficiencies in the existing process of developing galleries.

2. DEPARTMENTAL GALLERY PROPOSALS

The ECTF next designed a procedure for soliciting more detailed information about gallery requirements.* All curatorial departments were asked to complete a set of gallery proposal forms. A sequence of questions was posed, with the understanding that the relevance of particular questions would vary according to a department's collections and its approaches to presenting them.

The form asked for a general description of the galleries proposed by each department with particular reference to the nature of the collections, the purpose of the exhibit, the organization of space, and overall design. The same questions were also to be answered in detail for each individual gallery with additional sections on the content and support materials, the conservation and security needs, and specific design. Departments were requested to indicate minimum, medium, and maximum space requirements for each of the galleries, and to describe how the proposal would be affected if either the minimum or maximum figure was eventually allocated. The form also asked departments to show in what ways the proposed galleries would differ from the existing galleries, and which parts of the current galleries would be difficult to relocate.

The proposal form further requested a description of the relationships between a department's galleries and those of other departments, including any area of overlap, and an indication of which galleries the department would prefer next to its own. The final section asked for suggestions for interdisciplinary and general galleries, and for an account of any contribution the department would make to such galleries. In addition, departments were encouraged to submit ideas for the overall gallery plan. A sample gallery proposal form is included in Appendix D.

---

*The Gallery Proposal Form distributed to all curatorial departments September 1977 emphasized the conceptual rather than physical aspect of a "gallery". Although a lower limit of approximately 1,000 square feet was established for an individual "gallery", the basic approach to defining a gallery as outlined in the proposal forms was that a gallery consisted of any area in which a unified concept would be communicated, with sub-themes as described.

All curatorial departments submitted these forms, and groups such as the Discovery Room Working Group and Temporary Exhibition Committee also drew up proposals for galleries. A total of twenty-eight proposals was received.

To process all this information, the proposals were divided into groups, and each group was assigned to a team of ECTF members. The teams identified the areas that needed amplification and, where necessary, discussed the proposals with the department concerned.

The following facts emerged from this analysis:

- The total gallery space requested was far more than the space that would be available even in the expanded Museum.

- There were marked differences in approaches between the science departments and the art and archaeology departments, the former tending to emphasize their disciplines and the latter their collections.

- There was a desire for departmental gallery space of the traditional kind.

- There was a considerable number of ideas for interdisciplinary galleries.

- There were evident patterns of relationship between various galleries.

3. THE CLUSTER CONCEPT

Because the preliminary assessment indicated that the proposed galleries, as a totality, represented networks of interrelated concepts rather than isolated ideas, the ECTF produced charts showing how these interrelationships might be used to group the galleries into clusters. Bulletin #6 described these gallery clusters and provided a basis for discussions of the cluster principle as a possible approach to the overall gallery plan (Figures 1 and 2).

In the same bulletin, the ECTF outlined the initial results of its examination of the proposals for interdisciplinary galleries. Since there would not be enough space to implement all the ideas put forward, it was suggested that there could be short-term (three to six months) and medium-term (two to five years) as well as permanent interdisciplinary galleries. In this way, more ideas could be presented.

Examination of the proposals showed that some of the interdisciplinary galleries could be related to clusters of departmental galleries, while others were independent. Some of the ideas proposed spanned several clusters. The ECTF suggested that both cluster-related and interdisciplinary galleries could be either short-term, medium-term, or permanent.

The ECTF by this time accepted the following propositions as a basis for its subsequent planning:

- Clusters of galleries, as presented in the accompanying charts, should be made the basis for an overall plan of galleries.

- There was a need for a large Museum-wide (short-term) exhibition hall.

- Additional short-term exhibit spaces should be provided throughout the Museum in relation to the clusters. These could accommodate small temporary exhibits, either from inside or outside the Museum.

- Medium-term exhibit spaces were desirable to accommodate interdisciplinary concepts that warranted longer exposure than temporary exhibitions, but which would not be part of the Museum's permanent displays. Such galleries could be either cluster-oriented or Museum-wide.

- A third type of multi-disciplinary gallery was needed to accommodate permanent introductions for clusters of galleries.

4. CONSULTATION WITH GROUPS OF DEPARTMENTS (CLUSTERS)

To further develop the cluster idea, the ECTF again
established teams to meet with groups of departments to
determine the galleries to be included in each cluster,
the particular needs of the collections involved, and the
space and location requirements of each cluster.

The outcome of these meetings was as follows:

- There was general, although not unanimous, acceptance of
  the cluster concept.

- Some changes were made in the original composition of
  clusters (e.g., Canadiana was transferred from the New
  World to the European cluster).

- The Textile Department suggested that its galleries
  might be distributed among three clusters (the Ancient
  World, the Far East, Europe/Canada) so that its material
  could be integrated with that of other departmental
  galleries.

5. PLANNING FOR CLUSTERS: THE OVERALL PLAN

Pursuing the idea of gallery clusters, the ECTF devised
several possible arrangements of galleries. Space
allocations were proposed, taking into account the total
areas requested for each cluster and the total available
space. After discarding several plans, the ECTF distributed a Bulletin which presented two alternative arrangements for the gallery clusters (Plans A and B) and
specified the relative amounts of space allocated to the
clusters in each. Each plan was accompanied by a rationale
and by a list of advantages and disadvantages. The Bulletin
invited comments from all Museum staff to help the ECTF
make its choice.

There was a heavy response to the invitation, and a task
force team met with each cluster of departments to discuss
the implications of the two plans. As a result of the
general reaction, a third plan was drafted and posted for
comments.

As it was evident that none of the proposed plans was entirely satisfactory, the ECTF put forward further options. More discussions were held with the clusters of departments whose galleries would be affected by the new modifications. The departments responsible for administration and facilities were interviewed to find out their reactions to changes that would affect their areas of operation. There was also frequent consultation with the Project Office about alterations to the public facilities considered necessary by the ECTF. Altogether twelve different gallery plans were considered at one time or another.

It was particularly important at this stage to coordinate the ECTF's activities within the overall renovation and expansion programme. As gallery requirements were identified, the ECTF suggested changes to the Project Office. As it became clear that the space demanded greatly exceeded what was available, the Project Office had the building plan modified to provide more gallery space in prime locations. After all this discussion, the ECTF presented its chosen plan to the Director. The plan finally approved was a modified version of Plan A. The decision was announced and the ECTF began to develop the detailed cluster plans.

At this point, the ECTF had to consider the following factors and constraints (see floor plans in Figure 3):

● One gallery was permanent - the Vertebrate Fossils gallery.

● The Chinese Wall-paintings, the Ming Tomb, and the Totem Poles posed particular relocation problems.

● The configuration of the proposed building and in particular the amount of space available on different floors would determine the ways in which clusters could be located.

● The atrium areas would have to be limited to displaying materials which were not sensitive to light.

● The positioning of Exhibition Hall and of the cafeteria was a controversial matter.

● The case for a theme gallery was strong.

● It was desirable to distribute the documented public attractions throughout the building.

Figure 3: The Building and Some Specific Constraints

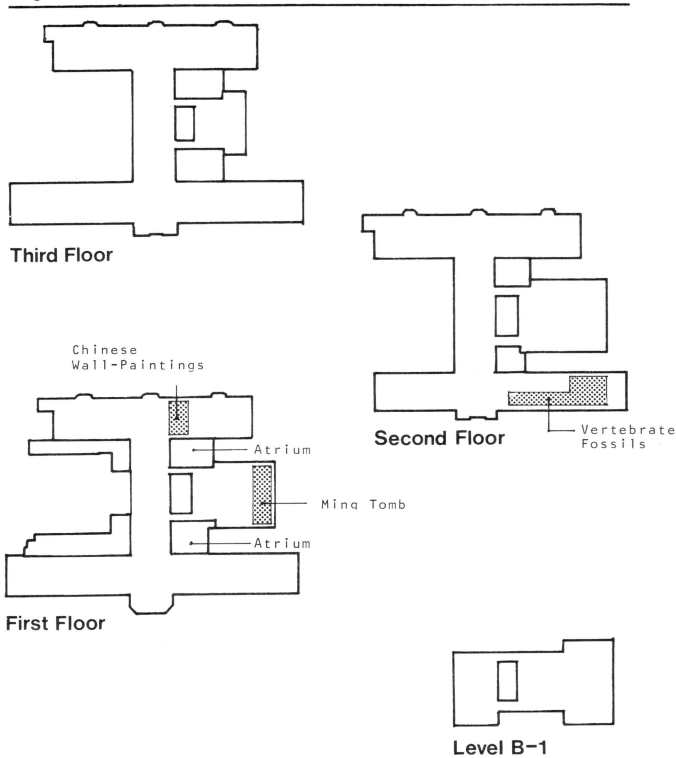

Third Floor

Second Floor

Chinese Wall-Paintings

Atrium

Ming Tomb

Atrium

First Floor

Vertebrate Fossils

Level B-1

● Conservation posed problems in relation to the building design. (The micro-climate workshop had not yet taken place.)

● Relationships between clusters could be established in different ways; e.g., Life and Palaeontological Sciences might be located on the same floor; alternatively, Life and Earth Sciences might be grouped together.

● At least one cluster would have to be divided because of space limitations and the configuration of the building.

6. PLANNING WITHIN CLUSTERS: DETAILING THE OVERALL PLAN

The final stage of planning for the detailed space allocations and the arrangement of galleries in clusters required considerable help from the curatorial departments. The ECTF teams helped the departments to decide what would be communicated by each cluster and what by the individual departmental galleries. Overall communication objectives were established for both the clusters and the individual galleries.

The preliminary planning of each cluster varied according to the degree of integration of the ideas involved. The most complete integration took place within the Ancient World cluster. (This was the name later given to the Mediterranean Basin cluster, which comprised West Asian, Egyptian, Greek and Roman, and Textile galleries.) The stages by which the Ancient World cluster was planned are described briefly below.

First, alternative approaches were considered. Then, three models were proposed for the arrangement of clusters in general (Table I). The second was the one adopted for the Ancient World.

The second stage was the organization of ideas as reflected by the actual collection strength. The results are illustrated by Figure 4, which shows the chronological relationships among the different regions of the Ancient World.

In the third stage, the chronology was portrayed by a number of time bands, each representing a significant period for which

departments would develop galleries. After the general time
bands were established, different physical arrangements of
these bands - each now representing a set of galleries - were
explored. The one finally adopted (Figure 5) determined both
the sequence of the sets of galleries and the logical
circulation route through them.

Using bubble diagrams (Figure 6), a sequence was established
for the galleries within each time band. When the order of
galleries was settled, a preliminary allocation of space was
made. After any necessary revision and refinement, the preliminary plan for the area was adopted. Simultaneously,
communication objectives for each time band were developed.

Table I: Alternative Approaches to Gallery Arrangements

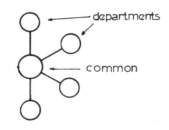

A.
One common gallery with
independent departmental
galleries fanning out from
it.

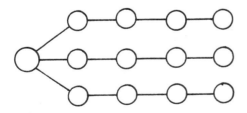

B.
Parallel development of
departmental galleries as
part of one comprehensive
statement.

C.
An integrated story with
no departmental galleries.

Figure 4: Preliminary Diagram of Chronological Relationships: Ancient World Cluster

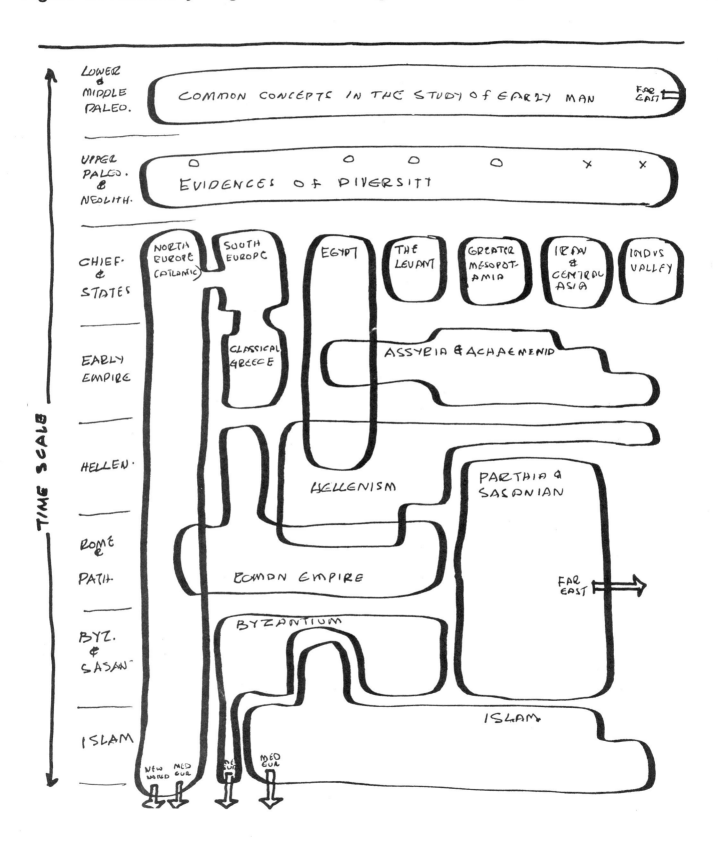

By the time this stage had been completed, a plan for the
development of the gallery area had been accepted by the
four departments involved. The curators' work had produced
an integrated concept which may result in an exciting presentation of the succession of cultural periods and of the
variations between geographical areas in the Ancient World.

There is now a preliminary plan for each cluster area (see
Part III B). Some plans are comparatively simple, others

Figure 5: The Time Bands

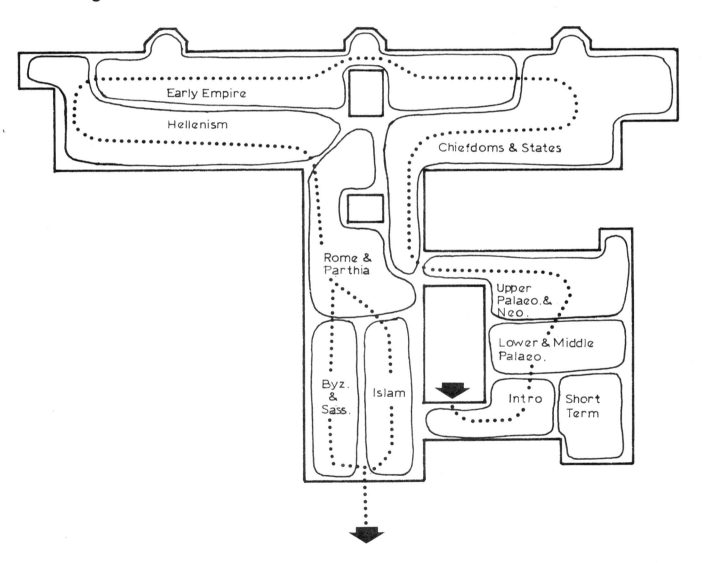

are more complex. All, however, show the general direction
being taken by departments concerned.

The overall gallery plan, which was the result of this process,
is discussed in detail in Part III. It is important to note
that because many people in the Museum were involved, the plan
is likely to have the necessary support and backing for its
effective implementation. In many cases, departmental thinking is far in advance of the present stage of planning.

Figure 6: Preliminary "Bubble" Diagram: The Ancient World Cluster

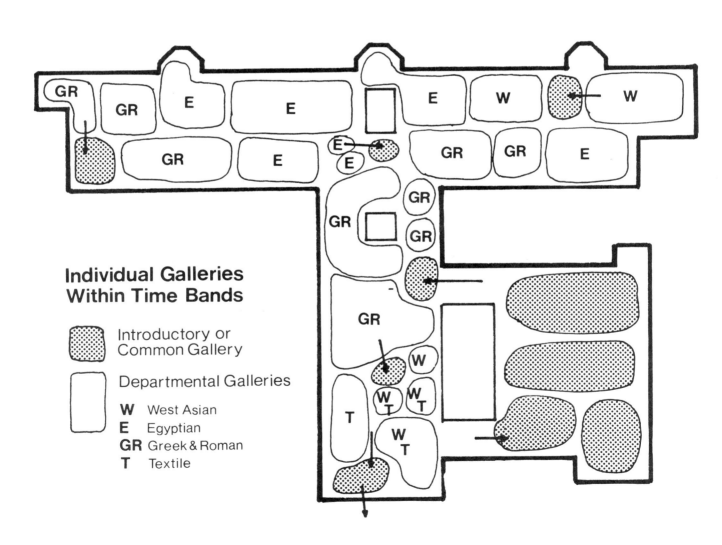

B. Visitor Survey and Gallery Evaluation Activities

1. INTRODUCTION

During both stages of the project, the ECTF carried out numerous visitor surveys and gallery evaluations in order to ensure that its plan would have a broad foundation of objective information. There were two main purposes to these studies: first, to establish a framework for the deliberations of the ECTF; and secondly, to provide the Gallery Development Teams with detailed information on how visitors use the Museum and its galleries. Accordingly, the ROM is now able to approach the planning of its galleries with accurate knowledge of the identity of its visitors, their expectations and perceptions of the Museum, and the effectiveness of various aspects of the exhibits as means of communication.

The surveys and evaluations undertaken by the ECTF were of two types. The visitor *surveys* were intended to provide broad statistical information about the ROM's visitors and how they use the Museum. The gallery *evaluations,* on the other hand, were aimed at discovering which parts of exhibits and galleries assist in successful communication and which do not.

Following are the studies completed by the ECTF. A brief description of each survey or evaluation is provided in Appendix E.

(1) Visitor Perception and Profile Survey

(2) Visitor Circulation Pattern Study

(3) Overall Visitor Tracking and Satisfaction Survey

(4) Discovery Room Evaluation

(5) Evaluations of Individual Galleries

(6)   "Dragon Throne" Evaluation

(7)   "Current Research" Case Evaluation

(8)   European Galleries Observations

(9)   Observation of Members' Tours

The ECTF believes that an understanding of the methods used to collect information and a knowledge of the results obtained would be of great interest and value to other institutions. The reports on the two main Museum-wide surveys (Visitor Perception and Profile Survey, Overall Visitor Tracking and Satisfaction Survey) and the complete report on the eleven individual gallery evaluations will therefore be published as the second volume of *Mankind Discovering*. The results of the Discovery Room Evaluation will be published in the full report on that project. Detailed reports on other individual surveys, the *Opportunities and Constraints* report, and the report on the micro-climate workshop will be published by the Museum in a monograph series.

Each of the surveys and evaluations was designed for a specific purpose. Consequently, some were done in greater detail than others, although structured sampling was always used. For example, the Visitor Perception and Profile Survey (VPP) was conducted over four days (both weekend and weekdays) during each month of a full calendar year. On those days, every tenth "casual" visitor over the age of five who entered the Museum was interviewed. Almost 5,000 interviews were conducted, which provided a substantial sample of the ROM visitor population. The individual gallery evaluations, on the other hand, were less comprehensive but were sufficient to test the communication effectiveness of these galleries.

Various survey techniques, singly and in combination, were used according to the purpose of the study. The four most frequent methods were administered questionnaires, visitor tracking, visitor counts, and general observation of behaviour. Questionnaires were used for the studies which required detailed information on visitors' thoughts and reactions. The questionnaire interview usually lasted five minutes or less. The tracking method consisted of observing the behaviour of a selected sample of visitors in a certain gallery. Both their paths through the area and certain forms of behaviour (e.g., stopping, reading labels, conversing) were recorded. The questionnaire and tracking methods were often combined. Counts were taken of every visitor who passed particular circulation points in order to discover the patterns of use of selected

Figure 7: Gallery Areas

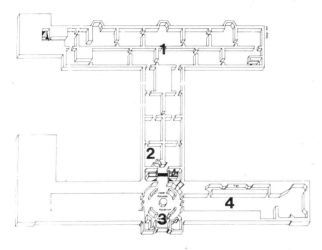

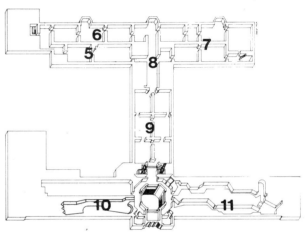

3RD FLOOR

1. Far Eastern
2. Islamic Arts
3. Special Exhibit - Rotunda
4. Mammals, Fish & Reptiles

2ND FLOOR

5. Textiles
6. Roman Life
7. Egyptian & West Asia
8. Classical Corridor
9. Greek & Roman (Early)
10. Invertebrate Fossils
11. Vertebrate Fossils

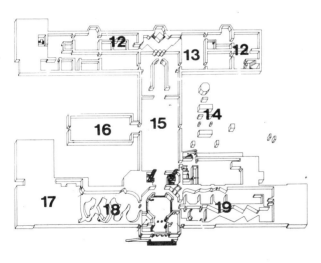

1ST FLOOR

12. European
13. Chinese Murals
14. Tomb Garden
15. Armour Court
16. Exhibition Hall
17. Planetarium
18. Mineralogy
19. Geology

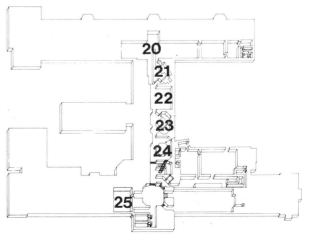

LOWER FLOOR

20. North American Cultures
21. African Cultures
22. Temporary Ethnology
23. North West Coast Cultures
24. Ontario Archaeology
25. Discovery Room

areas. In the fourth method, different forms of visitor behaviour were observed and recorded in a way similar to the
tracking method, but these latter observations did not involve
following a visitor through a designated area.

Since some galleries lack specific names, the committee
divided the Museum into a number of "gallery areas", identified by circulation routes or by content, in order to analyze
the tracking information in the Overall Visitor Tracking and
Satisfaction Survey (OVTSS). These areas, identified in Figure
7, will be used in future to refer to any unnamed galleries.

The next section presents findings from the surveys and
evaluations that have been especially useful in developing
the ECTF's overall gallery plan. Their significance should
become apparent as the Gallery Development Teams begin their
work.

2. A PROFILE OF THE ROM VISITOR

(a) SOCIO-ECONOMIC CHARACTERISTICS AND INTERESTS

The "casual" ROM visitor (any visitor who is not a member of
a school group or other organized group) is most likely to be
adult, well-educated, and English-speaking.

Observations showed that more than 75% of the casual visitors
were adults, 11.3% were adolescents, and the remainder were
children (6.8%) or senior citizens (4.5%). The maturity of
the ROM audience was even more noticeable if adults and
senior citizens were grouped together, because these categories
represented 81.9% of the visitors.

Visitors to the Museum are also characterized by the considerable amount of schooling they have received. Almost 50% have

had some form of post-secondary education. In fact, the proportion of visitors who have completed university education
(37%) is ten times the corresponding figure for Metropolitan
Toronto residents (3.7%), as reported in the 1971 census.*
Furthermore, the percentage of high school graduates among ROM
visitors is close to 80%, a much greater proportion than is
represented in the population of Metropolitan Toronto: the
1971 census indicated that only 10.4% of Toronto residents
have completed high school. The majority (87.3%) of the
casual visitors speak English in their homes. The 1976 census
reports only 55.7% of Metro residents in this language category.

The ROM currently appeals only to a limited segment of the
general population. Sections of the public not drawn to the
Museum include unaccompanied children, adolescents, senior
citizens, and ethnic minorities. It also seems that the ROM
does not appeal to adult members of the public who have not
completed secondary school. Other studies have shown that the
less well-educated public often feels intimidated by museums.**
If the ROM wishes to attract a wider range of visitors, this
concern must be reflected in the general attractiveness and
mood of the new galleries.

It was notable that a different kind of audience was attracted
to the ROM by the well-publicized exhibition "In the Presence
of the Dragon Throne". During this event, the number of Museum
visitors who spoke Chinese at home increased significantly
because a special effort had been made to inform the Chinese
community of the exhibition.

The present Museum audience appears to have acquired a certain
level of traditional learning skills. The ROM therefore has
an opportunity to offer its visitors information at a variety
of levels in its exhibits. It could present material ranging
from a broad outline of information to detailed and thought-
provoking questions.

---

*These comparisons with the Metropolitan Toronto population
 are based on the results of the 1971 census, excluding those
 under 4 years of age, as a detailed analysis of the education
 levels in the 1976 census is not yet available for the
 Metropolitan Toronto area.

**Manfred Eisenbeis, "Elements for a Sociology of Museums,"
 Museum XXIV, No. 2 (1972): pp. 110-119.

Occupations appear to be less important than age and schooling in defining the typical ROM visitor. In general, a wide diversity of occupations was noted. However, of all casual visitors, students comprised the single largest occupational category (29.4%). While most in this category (18.1% of all visitors) were children or adolescents, a substantial number of older students also visited the Museum. The next largest groups were professional (12.5%), sales, trade, or technical (10.1%), and homemakers (9.5%). It seems, therefore, that educated people find the ROM an interesting place to visit. The percentage of students may reflect the fact that one of the purposes of the Museum is to provide information complementary to their formal education.

The ROM is a museum of international reputation and is one of Toronto's tourist attractions. Its audience is drawn from a wide geographical area, with more than half the visitors coming from outside Metro. Tourist attendance, particularly from the United States, increases both absolutely and proportionately during the summer months, while Metro attendance decreases. From May until the end of August, the proportion of visitors who lived outside the Metropolitan Toronto commuting area increased from 29.5% to 46.3%.

The proportion of ROM visitors from the City of Toronto (27.3%) was found to be greater than the proportion of suburban visitors (21.2%), although the city's population is far less than the total Borough population. The remainder of the Museum audience came from the commuting area (15.1%), the rest of Ontario (12.6%), other provinces (4.4%), the United States (15.7%), and other countries (3.7%).

Very few people visit the Canadiana galleries. In fact, the number of visitors to Canadiana recorded during the survey periods was approximately 3.4% of the number recorded at the main building. Visitors to the Canadiana galleries differ from other Museum visitors; they are usually older, more regular in their visits, and more specific in their interests, and a larger proportion of them come from Metropolitan Toronto or its commuting area. The Canadiana galleries attract proportionately fewer American visitors than the main building, and tourist attendance does not increase in the summer.

Of the visitors to the Canadiana building, 93.8% were adults, as compared to 82% of those to the main building. There were 3% more senior citizens, who, according to the questionnaires, made up 11.6% of the Canadiana audience, compared to 3.9% at the main building.

The main building attracts a higher proportion of repeat visitors but more of the repeat Canadiana visitors had been within the previous year (70.3% as compared to 57.9%). Significantly, Canadiana visitors tend to go to other museums more frequently. The proportion of Canadiana visitors who had interests or hobbies related to the Canadiana collections was 10% higher than the proportion of visitors to the main building who had related interests or hobbies. More Canadiana material was the only change visitors consistently suggested as an improvement to the main building.

During the summer, the proportion of Canadiana visitors who lived outside Metro Toronto increased by 2%. While visitors from the United States made up 25% of the ROM's main building's clientele in the tourist season, they accounted for only 15% of the Canadiana building's.

The Canadiana galleries have the potential to attract more than their present audience. It appears, from the number of repeat visitors, that those who go to these galleries enjoy their visits.

(b)   FREQUENCY OF VISITS

Visitors to the ROM are "museum-goers". Most have been to the ROM before, but many have not visited in more than a year. About 20% are regular patrons. Many ROM visitors also go to other museums and art galleries. The ROM can therefore expect its public to have both an interest in viewing museum collections and some familiarity with methods of exhibit presentation.

Repeat visitors made up just over 66% of the Museum's attendance. Of these, 30.5% (representing 20% of the total ROM clientele), had made at least three visits in the past year, while 42% had not been in more than a year. The repeat visitors who had attended the Museum more than a year earlier and the first-time visitors accounted for 74.4% of the total attendance.

Eighty-four per cent of all ROM visitors had attended other museums within the past two years, and over 50% of this number had been at least three times.

Members formed only 3.7% of the casual visitor population. Many returned frequently, and more than 50% had visited more than eleven times in the past year.

(c)   INTERESTS OF VISITORS

Visitors to the ROM are usually interested in subjects which are associated with many museums. Their interests are wide-ranging and only a few subjects are especially popular with large numbers of people. Of all visitors, 45.4% had come without a specific reason. Among exhibits that people had come specially to see, the current special exhibition was mentioned by 20.9% of the visitors, the dinosaurs by 11%, the Far Eastern collection by 4.3%, and the mummies by 3.2%. Dinosaurs and mummies are perennial favourites of museum-goers, and the ROM's extensive Far Eastern collection is one of its more widely known and highly publicized attractions. No other individual item was specified by more than 3% of all visitors as something they came to see.

Even though ROM visitors may express an interest in certain subjects, they may well be curious also about other Museum exhibits. Visitors who came to see particular galleries, apart from the special exhibitions, were not usually motivated to seek out these galleries either exclusively or first. Moreover, those who mentioned that they had an interest or hobby related to the ROM did not indicate that they necessarily intended to seek out the corresponding collection. For example, while 10% had an interest in art, only 1.2% had come for that reason. Similarly, 3.2% were interested in antiques and furniture, but only 0.6% gave these as things they had come specifically to see. Evidently, the great variety of the ROM's collections is a strength which should be emphasized to appeal to the interests of the ROM audience and to the general public.

Even those visitors attracted to particular subjects were not usually specialists or dedicated collectors. The majority (54.1%) did not have an interest or hobby related to the ROM collections, and most of the remainder expressed only generalized interests (9.1% mentioned history, archaeology, or anthropology).

Most visitors who were collectors (32%), described their collecting in general terms, e.g., art or antiques, rather than Impressionist art or Chippendale furniture. The major emphasis of exhibit presentation should therefore be placed on the needs of the general visitor with lesser provision being made for the serious collector.

Visitors seemed to have more interest in art and archaeology than in science. These subjects predominated both among the exhibits visitors had come to see and in their related hobbies. However, in each instance, the ROM's image as a "history" museum may have biased visitor responses.

3. VISITOR EXPECTATIONS

(a) NATURE OF THE VISIT

Visitors expect a trip to the ROM to be a serious as well as a
pleasurable and sociable activity to which they are willing to
devote a good deal of time. This attitude presents the Museum
with both the obligation and the opportunity to provide them
with an enjoyable and worthwhile experience.

Visitors generally come with friends. Even apart from structured groups such as school classes, the Saturday Morning Club,
and special organized tours, a visit to the ROM is not usually
an individual activity. Of the total ROM attendance, 82.5% come
accompanied by at least one other person. More adults visit
the ROM with adult friends or relatives (43.8) than with children (31.8%). Few groups of either children or adolescents (6.9%)
come to the Museum as casual visitors.

Few visitors "drop in" to see the Museum. Rather, a Museum
visit is regarded by most people as an "expedition". Only 6.9%
stated that they had come to the ROM because they were in the
area. Many (35.4%) came to the Museum because they were tourists,
or were bringing tourists. A further 8.6% came because they felt
the visit would benefit their school activities or those of their
children. While the remaining 34.2% had planned a visit to the
Museum, they did not give a specific reason for coming on that
particular day.

Although visitors expect to learn, they do not expect the
Museum to provide a formal educational experience. Instead,
they look to the ROM to present its collections in a setting
from which they can learn. Interesting subject matter, specimens,
or artifacts, and attractive display, rather than educational qualities, were the reasons visitors gave for preferring particular
galleries.

ROM patrons also expect to find a congenial environment. Because
many (41.8%) indicated they had used the cafeteria, good dining
facilities ought to be considered an essential Museum service.
Comfort is another important aspect of a Museum visit. About 50%
of the suggestions for improvements concerned the visitors'
personal comfort.

Visitors came prepared to spend a specific and considerable period
of time. Fewer than 10% were uncertain about the length of time
they would remain in the Museum. Over half (60%) intended to

stay at least two hours, and 20% were prepared to spend three hours or more. A two-hour visit was the most frequent plan (32.6%).

The length of time visitors actually spend at the Museum corresponds closely to their intentions. While only two different visitor samples were used as a test, they were large enough to make the close parallel in their results meaningful. The proportion who stayed from one to two hours (43.3%) was the same as those who planned to stay that length of time. Similarly, the proportion who stayed more than two hours (29.7%) differed by only 2.5% from those who had indicated that this was their intention. The fact that visitors stay for quite lengthy periods is another reason for making sure that they have comfortable surroundings.

Most visitors (45.5%), aside from those who came for the special exhibitions, do not appear to plan for a specific type of museum visit. Even in a museum the size of the ROM, they come to see what the Museum as a whole has to offer. They tour the Museum extensively, entering many galleries but often spending most of their time in a few and remaining in the rest for five minutes or less. When they become interested in a gallery, they view it in depth. Subject matter and type of display, rather than the location of the gallery or the order in which they come upon it, determine these stops.

In fact, contrary to the findings of earlier studies, visitors do not spend less time or seem less interested in exhibits in galleries which are seen towards the end of the visit. For instance, the Mammals, Fish, and Reptiles gallery on the third floor was usually among the last visited, yet many viewed its exhibits thoroughly. It appears that all ROM galleries have the potential to attract visitors and stimulate their interests, whatever the content. Thus, increasing the available information would help visitors to know what to expect as they travel through the Museum, would provide them with the opportunity to select what they prefer to see, and would enable them to avoid subjects in which they have little interest.

(b)   THE PUBLIC IMAGE OF MUSEUMS AND OF THE ROM

Visitors have a general image of museums but do not have a specific concept of the ROM, although it is a unique institution in Canada. ROM patrons have a clear image of museums in general, as educational institutions where aspects of the past are preserved and displayed. When asked about the purpose of "this Museum",

50% said it was education and a further 42.4% indicated it was preserving and illustrating the past. These perceptions obviously apply to many other museums as well.

The wide range of subjects first-time visitors expect to see at the ROM is usually found also in other museums. The most frequently mentioned subjects were very general, e.g., "art" (11.8%) and "history" (10.6%).

The ROM is evidently regarded as a museum that is more concerned with showing objects that illustrate the past than with interpreting them or using them in a scientific way. Among things which ROM visitors expected to find and came to see, those related to art and archaeology were predominant. The tendency to focus on the historical aspects of the exhibits suggests that visitors are unaware that the ancient tools or rocks they see are linked to the Museum's current activities in expanding human knowledge.

Visitors do not connect the research activities of the ROM with its educational role. The Museum is seen to perform an educational function through the display of artifacts and specimens and the provision of related information. While 50% specified "education" as a purpose of the ROM, less than 3% considered education to be the type of work done by Museum staff. On the other hand, "display" and "providing information" or "guiding" were each mentioned as the work of the Museum staff by about 30%.

The ROM does not project the image of an active and dynamic institution. Although its collections and the services offered can be an exciting and meaningful resource for visitors, it is not necessarily one that the people who use it consult frequently (42.1% of the repeat visitors had not come within the past year). Only 11.4% of the visitors felt that the Museum functioned as a community service or cultural centre and 10.1% believed its purpose to be "entertainment". Only a small number came to the ROM to attend films or tours (2.8%), or to use its library (0.5%).

Do visitors see the research work of the Museum as a contribution to our understanding of today's world? The study shows that the public is not clearly aware of the ROM's involvement in continuing research. Less than 3% mentioned "research" by itself as a purpose of the ROM, though 32.4% thought that Museum staff were involved in "archaeological and research work". If visitors perceive the ROM's research activities at all, their view is limited. It is likely that research is associated in their minds with archaeological work, resulting in the display of the objects discovered. The evaluation of the recently installed Current

Research case has indicated that while visitors are unaware of the range of the ROM's research activities, they are interested in these activities when they are pointed out.

To clarify its image, the ROM must develop its strengths to a greater extent. In particular, it should increase awareness of the connections between its displays and its research activities and of their relevance to the visitor.

(c)   SATISFACTION AND FULFILMENT OF EXPECTATIONS

While visitors expressed general satisfaction with their Museum experience and positive opinions of the ROM and its galleries, they did not convey a sense of excitement in their responses.

The satisfaction visitors derive is closely related to their expectations, which are often ill-defined. People come for a "museum visit" rather than to see particular features or collections. Not having any very clear or intense expectations, they tend to make wide-ranging, non-selective visits. Presumably, many of them are not prepared to spend their time wandering in and out of galleries viewing displays in a cursory manner until they find a gallery that particularly interests them. Consequently, most are neither surprised nor excited by their visits. If the level of visitor satisfaction is to be raised, the Museum's image must be brought into sharper focus.

Visitors' preconceptions of the Museum were found to remain unaffected by their visits, except in two instances. The temporary exhibition "In the Presence of the Dragon Throne" and the Discovery Room changed expectations and resulted in great satisfaction. In both cases, the approach taken to displaying the material and imparting information resulted in a particularly attractive and dramatic presentation. Furthermore, the Discovery Room method, making objects accessible for the visitor's examination, is radically different from that used in other ROM galleries. Most of the permanent galleries do not sufficiently challenge the capacities of their visitors.

There is a certain incongruity between visitors' perceptions of the ROM as an educational institution and the degree to which their expectations are being fulfilled. Visitors consistently commented on the need for more information, a fact which suggests that the galleries are not satisfying their eagerness to learn from the collections.

Although visitors may not be primarily interested in their own comfort, noticeable discomfort can limit their enjoyment and inhibit their learning. While visitors considered the ROM galleries to be comfortable in terms of lighting and cleanliness, they generally found them too hot.* Also, their reactions to the Museum's public facilities (mainly the restaurant and washrooms) were not always positive. If visitors feel at ease in their physical surroundings, they are more likely to benefit from their visits, as well as to gain a favourable impression of the Museum.

Visitor satisfaction would increase if there were access to more and better orientation information based on a clear organization of the Museum. Each visitor could then select an itinerary which corresponded to his special interests. It is important that visitors understand the scope of the Museum and the extent and organization of the galleries, so that they can conduct their visit in a way which satisfies them.

4. HOW VISITORS USE THE ENTRANCE AND GALLERY AREAS

(a) ORIENTATION AND CIRCULATION

One of the first surveys conducted by the ECTF revealed that ROM visitors find the physical organization of the Museum confusing. The poor organization of the entrance Rotunda, lack of orientation information, and inadequate directions throughout the Museum were among the causes of the confusion. To counter this, the ECTF initiated a standard orientation system by renovating the entrance Rotunda (Figure 8). However, a consistent system of directions throughout the building has not yet been provided.

Observation of visitors entering the Museum indicates that the orientation needs of visitors vary according to their degree of familiarity with the Museum. For instance, the information booth is used more during the summer when there is an increase in first-time visitors.

---

*It should be noted that the evaluations from which this information has been obtained were conducted partly during the summer.

Figure 8: Rotunda and Entrance Area

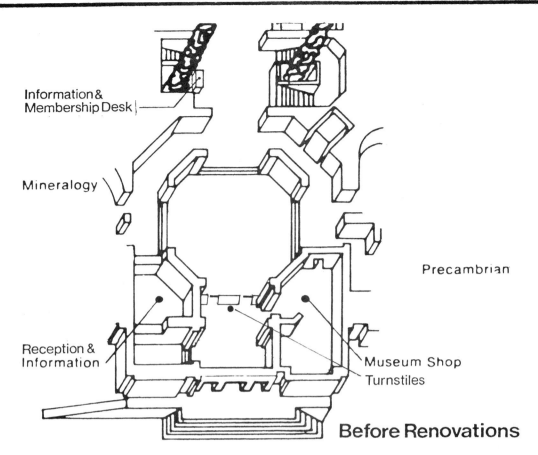

Information & Membership Desk

Mineralogy

Precambrian

Reception & Information

Museum Shop

Turnstiles

Before Renovations

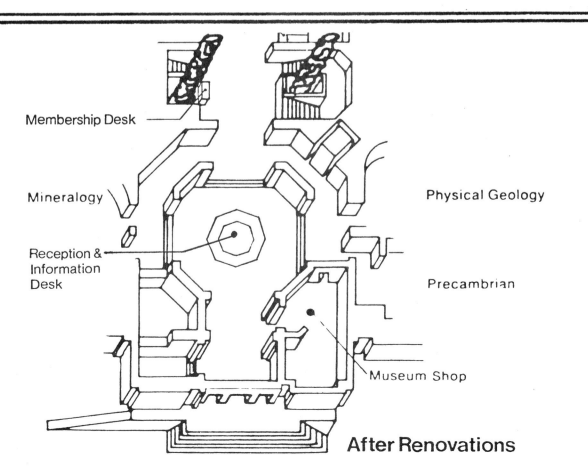

Membership Desk

Mineralogy

Physical Geology

Reception & Information Desk

Precambrian

Museum Shop

After Renovations

Understanding and making proper provision for visitor requirements enable better use to be made of public areas. Before
renovations were made to the Rotunda entrance, the space was
dominated by a bank of entrance and exit turnstiles and a
cashier's desk. The information booth was located in a remote
position near the stairs. Although 50% of visitors entering the
Museum appeared confused, fewer than 25% requested directions
either from the desk, the cashier, or from Museum guards. About
10% obtained maps.

To improve the entrance, the turnstiles were removed and the
cashier and information personnel were relocated at an octagonal
"island" desk in the centre of the Rotunda. These changes
lessened the confusion among visitors at the entrance. The proportion who used the information booth increased to 50%, with 34%
now obtaining a map. Furthermore, fewer visitors approached the
Museum guards; more appropriately, questions were directed towards
the reception staff.

The size of a reception area affects it efficiency. On crowded
days, the old Rotunda area did not provide sufficient space for
visitors to feel comfortable while pausing to make their plans.
Most come to the ROM with friends or family and soon after entering they must discuss what they are going to see first. A
crowded reception area frustrates or curtails such planning. If
the reception desk and orientation area are physically separated,
the confusion of "entrance hesitation" will probably be lessened.

Even after the improvements to the Rotunda, it did not provide
all the space needed by visitors for planning their visits. In
the new Rotunda area, 43% of the visitors stopped to confer, look
around, use their maps, or question a guard. However, 28% also
used the stair area directly ahead for orienting themselves, and
a further 5% used the Armour Court, the first gallery beyond the
stairs. Before the alterations, the Armour Court was used more
frequently for this purpose. With visitors now having information
available as they leave the Rotunda, the stairwell is used more
frequently for the "planning pause". Numerous directional choices
in the area also prompt visitors to made decisions there. In any
event, visitors need to spend their first minutes adjusting to
their surroundings, whether they are seeking information or merely
"getting the feel" of the Museum.

The large, open space of the Armour Court, visible from the entrance area, is a natural attraction which draws the majority
of visitors. After leaving the Rotunda, only 9% entered the
Mineralogy or Geology galleries on either side, 22% changed floors,
and 69% proceeded to the Armour Court. This contrasted with the

overall pattern of circulation on other floors, where visitors
entered the galleries off the Rotunda first. In comparison to
other exhibit areas on the first and second floors, the Mineralogy and Geology galleries had consistently low attendance even
though more visitors came particularly to see "rocks" than to
see the other exhibits on the first floor.

The area of the Armour Court presents the best opportunity for
the ROM to make a strong impact on visitors and to provide the
orientation they need. Here, a well-presented introduction to
the Museum's exhibits could help clarify the ROM's image for
visitors, and could provide them with a framework within which
to plan their tours.

ROM patrons usually tour the building extensively. Over 50%
saw five or more gallery areas covering a wide range of subjects.
The physical plan of the building, far more than anything else,
determines the overall circulation pattern. Visitors follow the
layout, floor by floor, from the first through to the third floor,
and then descend to the lower level. Therefore, a decreasing
number reaches each successive floor (63.3% reached the second
floor, 42.5% reached the third floor, and only 37.1% descended
to the lower floor). This pattern has been observed in other
museums. It is hoped that an escalator system will increase the
ease with which visitors change floors.

Where there is more than one level on any floor, the visitor
starts on the level he reaches first. On both the second and
third floors, visitors usually started with the east block galleries and then climbed the few stairs to the galleries in the
central block of the Museum.

Most visitors progress through the Museum horizontally. They
circulate from the front to the back, viewing a large portion
of a floor, and then return to the central staircase to change
floors. It follows that, whenever possible, connections in
subject matter between galleries should be made horizontally
rather than vertically.

Although visitors can find their way around, they seemed to find
the layout of the Museum confusing. Hence, extensive backtracking
and erratic movement patterns were often observed. Decision
points in the building are areas of confusion for visitors since
there is a variety of possible paths and few directions. Many of
the galleries that serve as circulation routes aggravate this un-
certainty. A high proportion of visitors en route to other areas,
passed through these galleries without stopping. In general,

visitors became disoriented in areas that functioned in more than a single capacity. A notable example is the Classical Corridor which is both a display area and a circulation route, and which contains six access points to other galleries. Consequently, visitors, uncertain of where they are, hesitate here and ignore the surrounding displays. Almost 90% of the visitors in the Classical Corridor did not look at the exhibits or scanned them only briefly.

Confronted with a choice of unmarked routes, a number of visitors simply reversed their paths or ventured only into the first gallery space of the wing. This behaviour was most noticeable at the junction of the central block with the west block on the lower, first, and second floors. Hence fewer visitors reached the extreme back parts of the Museum on these floors. Furthermore, in the west block of the Museum, visitors often toured either the north or south wing, but rarely both. These patterns could be influenced by visitor interests, though this influence would be diminished if the visitor became satiated with the subject or found the presentation monotonous. Ignorance of what to expect also curtails exploration. It is important to provide directions, particularly at points of choice, to give visitors assistance in getting their bearings and selecting their path.

The main stairway and adjacent Rotunda help visitors to understand the shape of the Museum. Most visitors preferred to return to this area to change floors rather than to use the back stairs. This finding confirms studies made at other institutions which describe the value of physical "landmarks". A distant view of a familiar landmark will orient the visitor more effectively than a sign that must be read from a short distance.

On all floors except the first, visitor attendance in galleries at the rear of the Museum was lower than in those closer to the main stairs at the front. To encourage attendance in the rear galleries, distinctive vistas or attractions should be provided which can serve as points of orientation.

The extent to which a visitor explores the ROM is affected by the company he is in rather than by any special interest. The most limited visits are made by those who come alone (usually adults). Almost 50% of these visitors saw only one or two galleries. Groups which included children toured more extensively. Twenty per cent of the groups consisting only of children and adolescents entered all the major gallery areas. In approximately the same amount of time, groups including children saw more of the Museum than did groups of adults only (a reflection, perhaps, of the shorter attention span of children).

Visitors wander into the galleries they encounter as they follow the physical plan of the building, rather than selecting galleries in advance. As already noted, apart from the current special exhibition, other galleries containing items which visitors particularly wished to see were not visited either first or exclusively. Evaluation of several individual areas, differing widely in subject matter and in location, also suggested this random quality in visitor circulation. Between 27.5% and 52.6% of visitors to all gallery areas except the Egyptian galleries stated that they had simply wandered into the area. Even excluding those who passed through a gallery area without stopping, almost 50% had no particular prior interest in the subject matter displayed. ROM visitors apparently progress from one gallery to the next, examining the exhibits that arouse their interest.

When visitors come to see the special exhibition, they focus most of their attention on that gallery. About 30% came specifically to see the Exhibition, and usually went there directly. Almost all of those who had seen only one or two galleries (23%) said that Exhibition Hall had been part of their visit. Furthermore, 25% of the visitors to Exhibition Hall spent between half an hour and an hour viewing its displays intensively. Another 8% stayed longer. The time and attention devoted to this gallery were greater than in others of comparable size. The way Exhibition Hall is used suggests that viewing the special exhibition is a major, and perhaps even exclusive, purpose for a Museum visit.

(b)   VISITORS' REACTIONS TO DISTINCT DIFFERENCES IN SPACES

While the configuration of the building requires circulation through the galleries, those galleries which act as main circulation routes encourage visitors to pass through them without stopping. For example, although most visitors to the ROM entered the Armour Court on the main floor, more than 25% passed straight through, and the others viewed the exhibits only cursorily. As already noted, a similar phenomenon was observed in the Classical Corridor on the second floor where 50% failed to stop, and a further 37% showed a low level of interest in the displays. Thus, in the design of galleries, it is necessary to consider their secondary role as circulation routes. Where possible, the use of alcoves (cul-de-sacs) to present certain aspects of the galleries would be more effective.

Multi-purpose areas can also create problems. For the special exhibition, "In the Presence of the Dragon Throne", a small introductory hallway was designed for display, for the distribution of information and brochures, and as the entrance and exit. The result was confusion and disorientation among the visitors.

The location of entrances and exits affects the flow of visitors through a gallery. For example, in the Sung and Yuan Ceramics gallery, the size of the gallery (1,200 square feet) and the arrangement of the display cases make the exit clearly visible from the entrance. Visitors often pass through this gallery without stopping.

Galleries that are physically separate and clearly identifiable are often viewed more intensively. For instance, a relatively large proportion of visitors examined many exhibits carefully in the Mammals, Fish, and Reptiles gallery (48.1%), Exhibition Hall (46.1%), and Vertebrate Fossils gallery (43.6%), all of which are self-contained, distinct spaces. While the subject matter of these galleries may have a special appeal, a comparison with the equally popular but undifferentiated series of Far Eastern galleries (where only 22.2% viewed the exhibits intensively) suggests that physical organization can affect visitor response.

The small, physically separate Rotunda Special Exhibit area on the third floor was one of the few galleries in the Museum where every visitor who entered looked at the displays. This occurred even though a complete change in display material (from astronomy to 18th-century textiles) was made during the study period. The placing of easily recognizable subject matter in a discrete space can encourage visitor interest.

At the same time, the physical organization of the Museum into a variety of spaces must not hamper visitors in understanding the relationships between the different areas. Movement through undifferentiated galleries without a unifying theme tends to limit the visit and the degree of interest in exhibits. For example, visitors spent little time in the Far Eastern gallery and only briefly examined its displays. The area occupies over 26,000 square feet and the average time visitors spent there was 15.3 minutes. Many toured only the south parts. In contrast, the physically separate Mammals, Fish, and Reptiles gallery is only a third the size, yet visitors spent an average of 18.3 minutes there and payed closer attention to the exhibits.

Visually striking spaces entice visitors to enter. The small,
mosque-like, introductory area to the Islamic Arts gallery causes
visitors to deviate from the tendency to choose a right-hand path.
On the second floor, when presented with simple doorways to either
a Greek pottery gallery on the left or a Greek sculpture gallery
on the right, 69% chose the right. At the same point on the
third floor, however, where the choice is between the Islamic
Arts gallery introduction area and the Early China gallery, 5%
fewer visitors turned right. Similarly, visitors were drawn
away from the expected path through the Far Eastern galleries
which would have led them past numerous small tomb figurines in
conventional cases. They gravitated instead towards the gallery
of the Chinese Temple setting, with its dramatic lighting and
composition.

Real or apparent cul-de-sacs can be intriguing for the visitor.
However, if they are not attractive they can be more easily ig-
nored than other areas. Galleries which are organized into culs-
de-sac and are also attractive, such as the Invertebrate Fossils
gallery, are very successful because visitors can comprehend the
space more easily and can clearly see the boundaries of the
gallery, and therefore they often view it in more depth. However,
because these dead ends do not form part of the main circulation
route, visitors can easily bypass them. For example, very few
visitors entered the isolated room containing the Continental
glass and porcelain collection, or the Lee Collection enclosure.
On the lower level, as soon as visitors were able to see the end
of the Mexican Cultural gallery, they turned back towards the
Rotunda.

(c)   GALLERY CONTENT AND IDENTITY

Visitors associate areas in the Museum with particular subjects
and with a particular location in the building, but they do not
distinguish galleries whose content is similar to that of
surrounding galleries. For example, the numerous European
galleries or Far Eastern galleries are identified by the visitor
as complete subject units. In the case of the Life Sciences,
the different subject concerns of the many departments are often
regarded by visitors as a unit, which they label "wildlife" or
"animals". Since visitors cluster galleries into mental groups,
it would be advantageous to match the overall physical organization of the Museum's collections with an appropriate conceptual
organization. Any such organization should both reflect and
clarify the relationships between subjects.

Obviously, the content and presentation of galleries are of
prime importance in arousing visitor interest. Yet, even after
viewing exhibits, some people were not aware of which galleries
they had visited. Arranging the galleries into large subject
matter areas appropriately presented, and providing information
on their content, would made it easier for the visitor to understand the organization of the Museum.

5.   COMMUNICATION EFFECTIVENESS

(a)   CREATING AN ATMOSPHERE FOR ENJOYMENT AND LEARNING

Any gallery has the potential to attract visitors, although
relatively few present ROM galleries do so. As we have seen,
visitors choose the galleries they view at random, though 25%
to 50% of them, after visiting a gallery, mentioned subject
matter as the reason why they were attracted to that particular
gallery. At present, however, few efforts are made to draw the
visitor's attention to a gallery and to introduce him specifically to its subject matter before entering. Unless this is
done, visitors may not notice a gallery entrance or, if they do,
may not be sufficiently interested to enter.

The importance of visual distinctiveness for ROM galleries was
noted in visitor reactions. The objects and displays that made
a strong impression were those that were clearly differentiated
from their surroundings. For instance, in the Early and Han
China galleries where many displays are composed of small
artifacts, the large tomb was the most popular exhibit.
Similarly, 25% of visitors to the Canadian Fish gallery were
impressed most by the largest lake trout ever caught.

Visitors noticed and responded to any distinctive treatment given
a gallery entrance. More then 10% of visitors to the Invertebrate
Fossils and Mineralogy galleries indicated that they were attracted
by the combination of display and signs at the entrances. While
the two galleries adjacent to the Rotunda are frequently missed,
the Mineralogy gallery has a substantially higher attendance than
the Geology gallery partly, at least, because of its visually
striking entrance.

Many theoretical and empirical studies on learning in the museum environment (Lakota, Shettel et al., Meyers et al., Washburne and Wagar) have stressed the need to orient the visitors to the material and organization of a gallery. The advantages of this approach are reinforced by the ROM studies. In most galleries, the majority of visitors were unable to discover either their purpose or organization and indicated they had not learned anything in particular from their experience.

Providing immediate indication of the purpose and organization of a gallery helps visitors to understand and appreciate its content. For example, 39.9% of visitors to the Invertebrate Fossils gallery accurately recognized its purpose as showing the origin and evolution of life forms. The concept of evolution was stressed clearly in the first display area, and almost 30% believed they had learned something about the subject. In contrast, most visitors to other galleries either mentioned purposes that were general and applicable to the ROM as a whole or simply named the obvious subject matter of the gallery. While these perceptions were not incorrect, the curatorial intent in most ROM galleries is to communicate specific ideas derived from the unique characteristics of the collections.

The design of a gallery is intended to help visitors understand the exhibits. If the organization is not made clear, the visitor can receive a distorted impression of the intended message. For instance, in the Vertebrate Fossils gallery, 11.4% incorrectly believed its purpose to be to show the evolution of man. The section dealing with human evolution, which is the first of the gallery's four areas, is apparently seen as introductory. Furthermore, visitors did not differentiate between the subsequent areas and usually thought that all of the specimens in the other units were dinosaurs.

Letting visitors know how the subject matter of a gallery is organized can decrease any initial confusion about how the displays are to be approached. Visitors expect to find an order underlying the display of exhibits. For the individual to proceed easily and confidently through a gallery, he must be told not only how it is organized but why it is organized in that particular way. For example, during the special exhibit, "In the Presence of the Dragon Throne", visitors had difficulty adjusting to the lack of sequential order in the exhibits. They did not realize that the order in which they viewed displays was unimportant here.

A logical gallery plan gives the visitor a context for his viewing, and it can be explained in an introductory area. Without being a preview of the exhibits, it can provide an

understanding of the material and the way in which it is
presented. Museum literature has discussed the advantages
to visitors of being able to relate acquired information to
some established framework. In the ROM, the context in which
a gallery is placed affects visitor reaction. The Chinese
Wall-paintings gallery is flanked by galleries displaying
European musical instruments and furniture, and mediaeval
sculpture. Despite the size and quality of the murals, over
50% of visitors went straight through the gallery without
stopping, while a further 24.4% glanced only briefly at the
work. Because of the abrupt change in subject matter and
type of presentation, visitors may not perceive the Chinese
murals as an exhibit at all. This faulty arrangement will
be corrected, and the Museum reorganization will place the
murals with the Far Eastern collections.

(b) CIRCULATION

The circulation paths through a gallery are created by the
floorplan and the arrangement of displays, and influence the
opportunities that visitors have to view and to appreciate
the collections. However, regardless of the established
routes, visitors followed individual and sometimes eccentric
variations, based on their degree of interest in the material
and the way in which it was presented (Figure 9).

Where alternative routes are available, it is important to
allow the visitor to select a route which corresponds to his
level of interest. Arrangements of display elements which
require unnecessary backtracking should be avoided. Such
arrangements may cause even highly interested visitors to
curtail their routes.

In the individual galleries evaluated in the ROM, there are
many possible circulation paths. Eight out of the eleven
galleries studied form part of a continuous route through the
Museum. In these galleries, wall cases, free standing displays,
and the location of entrances and exits determine circulation
patterns. The other three galleries are separate areas containing alcoves, in which most of the exhibits are ranged along the
walls.

The characteristics of each gallery affect the extent of circulation. Visitors moved more widely through galleries which
had imposed routes. In both the Vertebrate and Invertebrate

Fossils galleries visitors were channelled in sequence from one exhibit to the next through a narrow central path. Within this circulation pattern more than 50% of the viewers visited most parts of the Vertebrate Fossils galleries. Certainly the specimens (i.e., the dinosaurs) and the dramatic presentation were important, but the circulation pattern reinforced the other factors. Similarly, the downstairs displays of "In the Presence of the Dragon Throne" were designed to represent a street scene; the layout was therefore closed and restrictive. Visitors proceeded through the exhibit with ease. The upstairs part, on the other hand, was designed to create a court atmosphere, and the design was open and spacious, offering the

Figure 9: Examples of Circulation Routes in the Egyptian Galleries

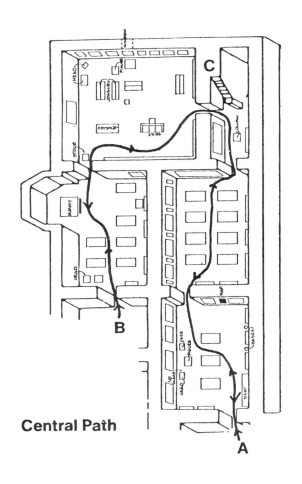

Central Path

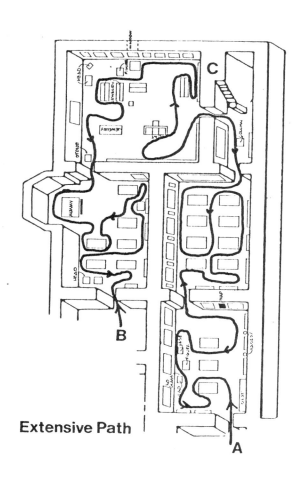

Extensive Path

individual a great deal of choice. Lacking information about
how to approach this arrangement, visitors sometimes hesitated
and backtracked. Nevertheless, a high proportion saw most of
the exhibit. Although interest is the main factor influencing
viewing patterns, clearly defined paths can strengthen visitor
response.

Even with only a casual level of interest, visitors can enjoy
and appreciate a gallery. Though 60% of the visitors to the
Canadian Fish gallery scanned the exhibits only briefly, 81.3%
indicated they had learned something.

Because each visitor will not be interested in every gallery,
the circulation path should be readily apparent for those who
do not wish to make a lengthy tour. At the same time the route
delineated should not encourage them to hurry past. An unob-
structed view of the exit from the entrance of a gallery leads
visitors to choose a direct path. Approximately 66% of the
visitors to the Early and Han China, the Islamic and the Sung
galleries went straight through without pausing. In these
galleries, exits are readily visible. If visitors can be drawn
into an exhibit area, and their attention caught by something
other than an exit, they have an opportunity to enjoy more of
the gallery. In a comparison of the Sung gallery with the
Ontario Prehistory gallery, for instance, more visitors (36.9%)
to the latter chose to follow a central path than did those to
the former (18.3%). The exits to both are easily seen
(Figure 10).

In the Sung gallery 69.3% of the visitors went directly from
one door to the next, while in the Ontario Prehistory gallery
only 39.7% followed this pattern (Figure 11). The positioning
of the display cases and the attractiveness of the diorama exhibit in the Ontario Prehistory gallery drew more visitors than
the arrangement of cases in the Sung gallery. Thus, a visitor
can be induced to follow a more extensive route by the positioning and presentation of the displays.

At the same time, a circulation route can be made clear by providing points in a gallery where visitors can easily make a decision. Perhaps the lack of any clear beginning to the displays
in the Sung gallery draws visitors towards the exit. The row of
cases acts as a barrier and visitors are unsure of the way to
approach it. Decision points without clues tend to confuse
visitors.

The capacity of a gallery affects the way in which an area is
viewed. Moreover, the presence of organized groups, particularly
school groups, affects the way in which other visitors view a

gallery. When casual visitors in the confined Vertebrate Fossils gallery encountered an organized tour, they either hastened past the group without looking at the displays or reversed their path. Furthermore, the noise level, which is usually increased in any gallery by organized tours, is further heightened here by the audio-visual aids.

On the other hand, in the more open spaces visitors felt at ease when encountering groups and would sometimes join the tour for a few minutes. In arranging the displays and routes through a gallery, therefore, groups, and in particular school tours, need to be accommodated so that other visitors will not be unduly distrubed.

Figure 10: Examples of Central Circulation Routes in Two Galleries

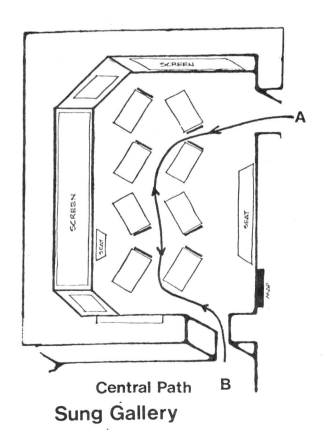

Central Path

Sung Gallery

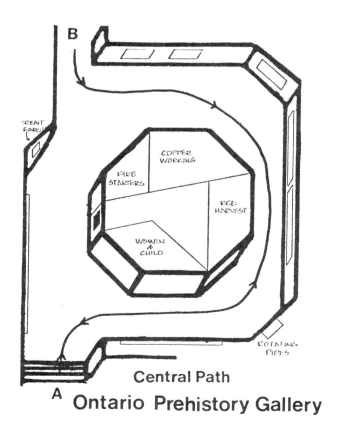

Central Path

Ontario Prehistory Gallery

In addition to organized groups, large crowds of casual visitors can affect viewing patterns in a gallery. Visitors to the Invertebrate Fossils gallery curtailed their stay when there was a large number of people present. Of the galleries evaluated, visitors considered this one to be the most "cramped" (as opposed to "spacious"), even though it is the same size as some of the other galleries. Adequate circulation paths must be provided in the more popular gallery areas.

The route established through a gallery can help the visitor to understand the organization both of the space and of the ideas. Size alone does not determine the visitor's ability to comprehend the spatial organization. The Islamic gallery is one of

Figure 11: Examples of Pass-through Circulation Routes in Two Galleries

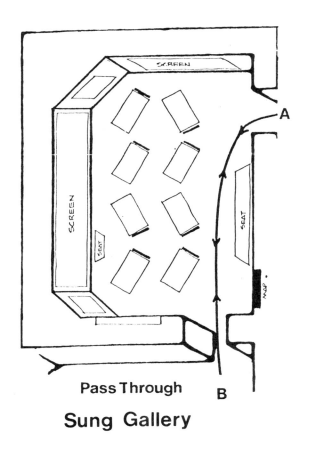

Pass Through

Sung Gallery

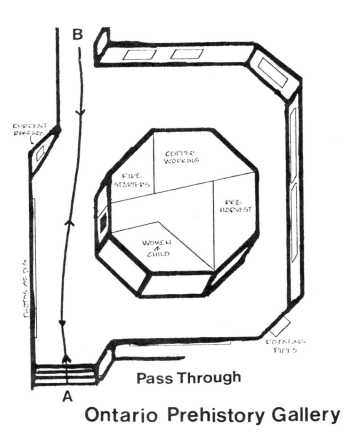

Pass Through

Ontario Prehistory Gallery

the smallest, yet it was one whose physical layout visitors had most difficulty in grasping. Of the visitors to the gallery, 15% suggested improvements to the sequential presentation and organization (a higher proportion than for any other gallery). In a gallery where the circulation route was clear (Vertebrate Fossils gallery), or where there was an evident match between organization of ideas and space (Invertebrate Fossils gallery), no improvements were suggested. The Sung gallery although its spatial organization seems simple had the second largest proportion of visitors who suggested improvements in its arrangement of displays.

The ECTF's studies, along with those of Neal, Meyers et al., and Shettel et al., show that there are advantages in reinforcing the conceptual organization of a gallery with corresponding physical subdivisions or sequences. All found that galleries with this type of reinforcement were less exhausting for the visitor, who did not have to spend most of his time trying to order the ideas for himself. It appears that learning is assisted if the content is placed in a rational sequence.

(c)   PRESENTATION AND COMMUNICATION

All display elements must enhance the subject matter in order to convey information effectively to the visitor and to increase his satisfaction. ROM visitors come not only to see the artifacts and specimens but also to learn something about them, and they are conscious of the way in which they are presented. The galleries that they preferred were generally those they considered the most informative. Visitors consistently suggested more or better presentation of information as an improvement to individual galleries, regardless of the amount already provided. They further indicated that the design of the displays required improvement. The galleries which seemed least popular and to which the highest proportion of visitors said they would not soon return (Textiles, Islamic Arts, and Canadian Fish) were also the ones where there was the highest proportion of recommendations for improvement.

The careful coordination of display elements, artifacts, and information is vital to a gallery's success. Although it is difficult to achieve, the results can be spectacular and rewarding as illustrated by "In the Presence of the Dragon Throne". Here, a high proportion of visitors not only saw the entire exhibition, spending a considerable amount of time there, but also understood the overall organization, were enthusiastic about the collection and its presentation, and were able to recall specific information. The permanent gallery most enjoyed by visitors was the Vertebrate Fossils gallery. While the material in both these exhibits was dramatic, the presentation highlighted the unique qualities of the textile artifacts and fossil specimens on display.

Visitors may not be uniformly drawn to all the subjects contained in the ROM, but galleries can be developed in ways which nonetheless invite an interest. A key element in attracting and maintaining interest is the use of variety and drama in the presentation. Clearly such techniques must be applied with caution. If a display is eye-catching but overly dominating, the impact of the artifacts or specimens themselves may be diminished.

However, dramatic features do have a powerful role to play in attracting visitors to a gallery. Without them, a visitor may ignore an entire area. For instance, 90% of the visitors to the Sung and Yuan Ceramics gallery did not even pause, and the rest viewed the displays only briefly. Of all the galleries evaluated, visitors rated this one the most "boring" (as opposed to "exciting"). It is not surprising, then, that over 75% could not specify a favourite aspect but referred only to the artifacts in general. This reaction is due in part to the unimaginative display of a great number of similar objects (in this case, Chinese ceramics).

Visitors are more fascinated by exhibits that incorporate dioramas or life settings and live exhibits. Large numbers of visitors to the Ontario Prehistory gallery (41.6%), the Vertebrate Fossils gallery (36.9%), and the Invertebrate Fossils gallery (38.2%), where either or both of these methods are used, mentioned these as the best-liked features of these galleries. Such forms of presentation are successful and popular because they provide an easily understood context for artifacts or specimens, and because they are different from the usual type of display. Although these particular techniques cannot be used in all galleries, the principle of creating a vivid setting for the exhibits can increase the visitor's interest.

Providing information that satisfies the visitor's curiosity contributes to his enjoyment. Once attracted by artifacts or specimens, or by their presentation, he may want to learn something further about their meaning. The many requests for more or different information and the general rating of the information provided as "too little" rather than "too much",

illustrate this desire. Moreover, visitors are interested in
reading material. In galleries evaluated, over 70% of visitors
indicated that they had read some of the information available.

If carefully composed and offered, didactic information need
not detract from the objects nor overwhelm the visitor.
Visitors take time to read information if they are interested
in the objects. During "In the Presence of the Dragon Throne",
for example (where 44% stayed more than half an hour), 62%
read the labels. Most visitors found them helpful in reinforcing what they had learned from the exhibition.

It is important that such information be easily visible and
that it relate clearly to the artifacts or specimens. The
evaluation of the special exhibition mentioned revealed that
visitors sometimes had difficulty in finding labels, in matching them to the appropriate items, and in reading them when
the light was poor. The key system of matching numbers to
artifacts caused confusion, especially when two different key
systems were placed next to each other. In the Vertebrate
Fossils gallery, visitors were frustrated in their attempts
to read an extended text panel from left to right, while the
display is viewed from right to left.

Different types of information will interest different visitors.
It is important to realize that the information visitors may
find appealing may not be considered the most significant from
the curatorial standpoint. For example, in a display on
current research, the curators involved wished to made visitors
aware that important information can often be derived from un-
prepossessing objects. From the way in which the information
was presented and interpreted, however, visitors learned how
to manufacture the object instead of absorbing its archaeological significance. Thus, the curators' primary goal was not
attained.

Similarly, highly technical information needs to be presented
carefully so that the visitor will recognize the reason for
it and can decide whether he would like to pursue it without
feeling intimidated. After all, the ROM studies showed that
few visitors are dedicated collectors interested in detailed
technical information.

In the Mineralogy gallery, more than 25% of the suggested
improvements had to do with the need for more information and
less technical labels. This gallery, where approximately one-
third of the exhibit space is devoted to detailed and technical
material, was the only one in which the labels were criticized

as being too technical. (Information does not need to be
simple-minded in order to avoid being overly technical).

Visitors appreciated the use of audio-visual techniques in the
Vertebrate Fossils gallery. While most (84.6%) read some of
the texts 67.1% indicated that they had viewed some of the
audio-visual screens, which they considered more informative.
Although the specimens were the main attraction, 10.7% of
visitors specified the audio-visual aids as their favourite
aspect of the gallery. When the overall presentation in a
gallery is stimulating and attractive, audio-visual aids need
not detract from the exhibits or written information.

The use of reconstructions and models can also be helpful if
reasons for their use are evident. For example, in the
Invertebrate Fossils gallery, 64.7% of the visitors were aware
of the comparisons made between real specimens and recon-
structed models and understood their function of presenting a
better description of an incomplete fossil or of one unavailable for exhibit.

In some cases, explaining why objects are displayed in a particular way can avoid negative impressions. For instance,
signs in a special exhibition informed visitors that lighting
levels were designed to protect the costumes and to create an
authentic effect. Almost 80% were aware of these purposes and
indicated they liked the lighting. Its use to create an
atmosphere that will enhance the artifacts or specimens is
important in the overall impression made by a gallery. When
care was taken in designing the lighting for these ends, the
majority of visitors liked the effects.

The security requirements of open displays must also be considered. While this method can be particularly appropriate to
certain artifacts, distinct psychological or physical barriers
may be needed for their protection, especially when such objects
are positioned in the middle of a circulation route.

Visitors are often curious about the feel and texture of
exhibits as well as about the way they function. In the
European galleries, openly displayed items such as chairs, doors,
and chests were frequently touched. The inconsistent use of
"Do Not Touch" signs appeared to confuse visitors, since they
did not realize that the restriction also applied to objects
not situated close to the sign. An unambiguous indication of
the behaviour expected must therefore be given.

Visitors learn from exhibits in a variety of ways. Although

didactic information is important, it is not the only way to
assist learning. In the comparison of the galleries evaluated,
there was no consistent relation between the proportion of
visitors who had learned something and the proportion who had
read some of the information. Artifacts or specimens presented in a context (e.g., habitat or diorama) may convey
their own kind of information. Even people who had wandered
slowly through a gallery without reading labels often felt
that they had absorbed something about the subject.

This section of the report has summarized the information from
the evaluation programme which directly concerns the development of the overall plan. However, the scope and the detail
in the full evaluation reports will be invaluable when development teams begin planning individual galleries.

C. Conservation and Micro-climates

Early in its consideration of display requirements, the ECTF
realized that the approach taken to the conservation of artifacts could have a dramatic effect on the overall plan for
galleries. The renovated and expanded Museum building is to
have an environment with a temperature range of 70°-76°F (21°-
24°C), and relative humidity between 25° and 50°. Currently,
both temperature and relative humidity (RH) vary widely throughout the year.

The main factor limiting increase of the RH above 25% in the
winter is the physical fabric of the old building, in particular, the wall construction. RH above 25% can seriously affect
the structure unless elaborate and costly precautions are taken.
The new wall construction in the Terrace galleries will be able
to sustain the difference in RH. Where an environment is provided adjacent to an outside wall of the old building (except
Exhibition Hall), the RH may not be greater than 25% in the
winter; in the new Terrace building under the same circumstances, it can be allowed to reach 35%.

The major conservation question raised by both the ECTF and the
conservators was: how would very sensitive artifacts (those
which needed closer climate control) be handled? Whatever base
conditions might be made available in the building, some type
of micro-climate would be necessary for certain artifacts, i.e.,
an environment, large or small, which would be self-contained
and isolated from the overall building environment.

The ECTF decided to sponsor a workshop to bring together conservators and other specialists from centres in Canada and the
United States to assist the ROM in determining how to deal with
the conservation requirements of its collections. In preparation, the following documentation was assembled:

- a review of the current methods of conservation;

- background information on the mechanical systems of the future building;

- an analysis of the varying sensitivities of the ROM's collections.

It was found that a small but important portion (10%) of the ROM's collections required micro-climates. Care of artifacts sensitive to moisture, light, and dust could be more efficiently managed through the provision of micro-climates than by an increase in the base level of climate control within the Terrace galleries. By this means, greater flexibility both in the types of climate that could be provided and in the arrangement of galleries would be made possible.

The workshop confirmed this approach. Micro-climates would be designed to create a special environment for the artifacts only rather than a blanket environment for displays and visitors. It also became clear that this approach would result in substantial energy and cost savings, a recurring theme in the subsequent workshop discussions of micro-climate solutions.

The workshop determined that although some methods currently practised in conservation could be applied at the ROM, the provision of novel types of mechanical equipment was necessary for adequate protection. The workshop participants successfully lent their efforts to defining the specifications for such equipment, and the ECTF is confident that proper care can be provided for all artifacts, even particularly sensitive ones, through the development of mechanical solutions.

A summary of the main conclusions and decisions of the workshop follows:

THE BUILDING

- Environmental improvements made to the Museum building in the course of the renovation and expansion programme will be adequate for the care of a large proportion of the ROM's collections.

- The outside walls of the new Terrace galleries will be built to provide greater resistance to moisture transference than is economically feasible for the old building, apart from the new Exhibition Hall.

- The new Exhibition Hall will give an extra vapour barrier added internally. This will allow the entire hall to be developed as a micro-climate, thereby providing additional flexibility for the display of exhibits with sensitive materials.

- In the atria, the environmental conditions will be the same, in general, as the base environments throughout the building, but the high light levels will restrict the use of these gallery areas to materials that are not light-sensitive.

- It had been suggested that live birds might be exhibited in an atrium area. Any area used for this purpose would need its own separate micro-climate.

- Any plan to use live plants in the building will need to be carefully considered because of the bacteria, insects, and particulate matter which they carry.

CHANGEOVER TO NEW CONDITIONS

- Standards for regulating the changeover from existing environmental conditions will be established by the Conservation Department. It will be necessary for the change to occur gradually as a great deal of damage to artifacts can result from rapid changes in the environment. Similar procedures will be used in changing over from summer to winter operations: the changeover from air conditioning to heating (and vice versa) must be gradual.

- The new environmental conditions will probably make the Museum much more attractive to pests. The fumigation facilities being built into the new mechanical systems for the building should deal adequately with this problem.

MICRO-CLIMATES

Buffers

- The conventional means of providing micro-climates is through the use of buffers. Silica gel, the most commonly used desiccant, may be employed as a buffer in conjunction with a means of drying or humidification. However, it is practical only on a small scale because of its maintenance requirements.

- Organic materials (e.g., wood) are useful in buffering climatic change. Such materials can be used for case construction, flooring, or panelling within a case.

- The use of buffers must be determined by individual micro-climate needs.

New Solutions

- In exploring new solutions, there were two aspects of micro-climates to be considered: the mechanical equipment for creating the environment, and the enclosure or case.

Equipment

- Large micro-climates (e.g., several period rooms grouped together in one wing) will be dealt with as an extension of mechanical systems for the whole building.

- Smaller micro-climates will require independent mechanical systems.

- Prototype equipment is being proposed for three scales of micro-climates:

  - 10-50 cubic feet

  - 100-200 cubic feet

  - 400-100 cubic feet (up to the size of a small period room or habitat).

- Table II illustrates the types of equipment which will be required for varying conditions.

- This equipment will be designed to meet acceptable standards with respect to:

  - noise levels

  - vibration generation

- electrical requirements
- water and drainage requirements
- in-case space requirements
- grille requirements
- access requirements
- cost requirements
- portability

Table II: Micro-climate Requirements

	Humidification[*]	Desiccation[**] (drying)	Cooling[***]
10-50 cubic feet	X	X	
100-200 cubic feet	X	X	X
400-1000 cubic feet	X	X	X

[*]Equipment to increase relative humidity from a base climate of 25-50 RH to a controlled climate of 50 RH.

[**]Equipment to decrease relative humidity from a base climate of 25-50 RH to a controlled climate of 20 RH.

[***]Equipment to decrease temperature from a base climate of 70° -76°F. (21° -24°C.) to 55°F.(13°C.).

Display Cases for Micro-Climates

- Display cases for micro-climates at the three previously outlined scales will be designed together with the equipment needed for the required climates. The cases will be as airtight as possible. A low leak rate is essential for energy and cost savings.

Lighting

- Lighting levels established by the Conservation Department must be adhered to.

- All lighting sources must be outside the micro-climates.

- Equipment for micro-climates will be designed to deal with radiant heat ("green-house effect") from external lighting sources, and with changes in the level of lighting from day to night.

- If incandescent lamps are used, they should be of low voltage because low level lamps create less heat in relation to the amount of light.

Mixing of Materials

- Mixing of materials with different conservation requirements in one display will have to be dealt with on an *ad hoc* basis. There are too many potential combinations to make a single approach possible.

Monitoring and Operations

- Monitoring and control of micro-climates will be the exclusive responsibility of the Conservation Department.

- A simple alarm device (both audible and visible) will be built into micro-climate equipment to signal a malfunction.

- Access to micro-climates must be controlled by the Conservation Department.

D. The Basis of the Overall Gallery Plan

The development of a plan that reflects the needs, concerns, and aspirations of some twenty curatorial departments and of a number of other departments directly concerned with galleries is a difficult objective to achieve. Conflicting demands require many compromises. Nevertheless, the ECTF attempted to make judgments which would benefit the Museum as a whole. Its goal was to produce a plan, comprehensible to visitors, which would provide the ROM with an image befitting its unique qualities and would enable the curators to present their collections and to communicate their ideas effectively.

In order to bring the proposed galleries into a unified scheme, a subgroup of the ECTF was formed to explore the possibility of a theme for the Museum. This subgroup eventually proposed a theme which was approved by the Director and adopted. The theme became a point of reference to which the ECTF has returned at many stages in its deliberations. The importance of its role is reflected in the fact that there will be a central gallery area to express it, and it will, we hope, continue to guide the gallery development teams in their work.

The theme is as follows:

"The Royal Ontario Museum exists to advance and create knowledge and understanding by discovering and preserving the record of nature through countless ages and the arts of man through all the years."

A short form – Mankind Discovering – was later agreed upon for promotion purposes. The Theme Working Group believed that the theme "should provide a unifying link for the Museum's diverse activities, reveal the function and purpose of different parts of the institution, explain and emphasize to all why and how such a diverse and heterogeneous place is and can continue to be a great and vital thing, and assist in a basic understanding to staff and public alike what the Museum is really about and what it seeks to do". Further they stated that "the theme 'Mankind Discovering...' would help to integrate in a flexible and subtle manner the displays and galleries of the Museum...".

In order to make the organization of the Museum more comprehensible to the visitor, the ECTF examined the visitor surveys. One important finding - that visitors move through the building in a methodical way, covering an entire floor before moving on to the next one - became determinative in its planning. Conceptual links between galleries can best be made if they follow established visitor movement patterns. If such links are established on the same floor rather than between floors, therefore, they are more likely to be understood by the visitor. Thus, closely related galleries were arranged together on the same floor where possible.

Examination of the gallery proposals revealed a pattern of relationships and led to the recognition of clusters of related galleries. The clustering principle provides not only opportunities for strengthening ties between departmental galleries where these are wanted, but also a means for communicating them easily to the visitor. The clustering of related galleries was a crucial consideration in organizing a number of gallery proposals into a single plan.

The cluster idea will not only make the Museum more comprehensible for the visitor but will also provide chances for the curators to communicate shared ideas which might otherwise remain unexpressed. The ECTF has attempted to provide many opportunities for realizing these aims in the plans. For example, the design includes a Museum-wide gallery, Mankind Discovering, which describes and illustrates the collective activities of the ROM. A series of temporary galleries will also increase the occasions for presenting new collections and ideas.

Current galleries do not reflect the vital, research-oriented activities of the ROM. Studies have revealed that visitors arrive with a certain idea of museums in general, rather than a specific image of the ROM, and that they depart with that view intact. Planning has proceeded on the assumption that the galleries should reinforce the unique qualities of the institution - both in its collections and in its curatorial staff - rather than attempt a broad coverage of all areas within the disciplines represented. The curators are frequently

specialists. For instance, the West Asian department has done
much field work in Iran, and this is reflected in the gallery
plans for the department. While the sciences are more often
able to present broad pictures of their individual disciplines,
curatorial expertise in specific areas will also be shown in
these galleries.

In the reorganization of the Museum some obvious constraints
made themselves felt, the most serious being that the departmental requests for gallery space were far in excess of what
would be available within the expanded Museum. Although gallery
space will be approximately 212,000 square feet (an increase
from the present 154,000 square feet), total requests exceeded
300,000 square feet. Thus a limit has had to be placed on the
number of ideas to be expressed and the amount of material to
be displayed.

The configuration of the available space (affectionately referred to as the "pregnant H") was in itself a serious limi-
tation on the possible arrangement of galleries and on the
circulation patterns that could be developed. A large open
space would have provided more freedom in accommodating the
complex set of galleries required to present the ideas and
display the material.

The time available for drafting the plan was also limited.
The process of consultation and investigation was slow. A
plan that attempts to reflect the varied and often conflicting
views of the staff requires much consideration, and will still
contain imperfections. Allocating space for Museum-wide
galleries rather than departmental galleries involved complex
negotiation and arbitration. Still, the ECTF believes that the
process itself creates a climate capable of surviving the imperfections of the original plan, and of generating a spirit
that seeks constantly to surpass previous accomplishments.

Part III
The Plan

Part III
The Plan

A. Description of the Overall Gallery Plan

In this section, the overall gallery plan is discussed briefly and is illustrated by the accompanying set of floorplans. Most of the areas available for galleries are within the existing H-shaped building, but there is one new gallery area - the Terrace galleries - proposed for the existing north courtyard.

The Rotunda will continue to be the main entrance. The restaurant and cloakroom facilities will be located off the side of the Rotunda and the control point to the galleries will be at the west end. A new group-entry area for students will be built at the B1 level.

The new Exhibition Hall and the adjacent atrium area will serve as the main short-term exhibition area. Additional space for temporary galleries will be included in each cluster.

The atrium next to Exhibition Hall will contain an access ramp to the Planetarium galleries.

The Earth Sciences will be situated on the first floor in the southwest wing and in the adjacent atrium area.

The Far East cluster is also on the first floor and will include the Terrace galleries, the northwest wing, and the two atrium areas flanking the Terrace. The Ming Tomb and the Chinese Wall-paintings will now become integral parts of the Far Eastern galleries.

The second floor will be devoted entirely to the Life and Palaeontological Sciences. There will be a large inter-disciplinary gallery and a series of departmental galleries.

The third floor will include the Ancient World cluster galleries and the main component of the Europe/Canada cluster. A conceptual link between these will be provided by continuing the chronological presentation of the Ancient World into the mediaeval displays of the European gallery.

The B1 level will contain the New World cluster galleries in the east portion of the central and Terrace gallery. The west portion of the central block will be devoted to the Old World Ethnology galleries.

The west portion of the Terrace galleries will house the remainder of the Europe/Canada galleries, including some European specialty collections, as well as the Canadiana and some Textile galleries. These galleries are arranged so as to enable a common area to be developed for parts of the Canadiana, Ontario Archaeology, and Woodland Indian galleries.

The B2 level will contain the Discovery Room and a children's participation area.

When completed, the new gallery arrangement will be a dramatic contrast to the present one. There will be an increase in the amount of gallery space and the redistribution of space will provide a better balance between the art and archaeology and science galleries. The science galleries, excluding the Planetarium, currently occupy approximately 28% of the total gallery space; the proposed allocations will increase this proportion to about 38% (excluding major common gallery spaces - Exhibition Hall, Mankind Discovering, Discovery Room).

Almost all galleries will eventually be relocated. The only gallery areas which will remain largely unchanged are the Dinosaur gallery on the second floor, and the room containing the Chinese Wall-paintings on the first floor. The Ming Tomb, now in the garden, will be situated within the Terrace galleries. The complete plan reflects the ECTF's attempt to make space allocations based on the collections and activities of departments rather than on historical precedent.

There will also be new kinds of galleries. The major theme gallery, Mankind Discovering, will make a comprehensive statement of the Museum's theme and will serve as an orientation and introduction to the Museum. A new permanent Discovery Room will replace the experimental one opened in July 1977. In addition, greater emphasis will be placed on temporary exhibits. In each cluster, space will be available for departments to develop temporary exhibits on new findings or material, and for the ROM to present displays lent by other museums to complement the clusters.

The present galleries, representing about twenty departments, will be replaced by seven clusters which will contain galleries from related departments, and will frequently include introductory and common display areas.

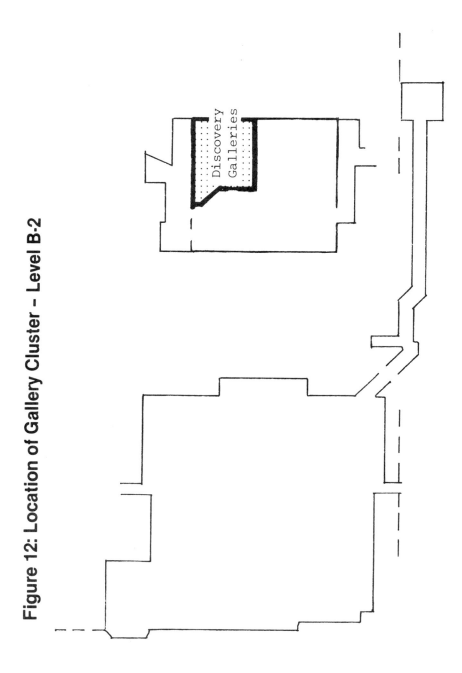

Figure 12: Location of Gallery Cluster – Level B-2

Discovery Galleries

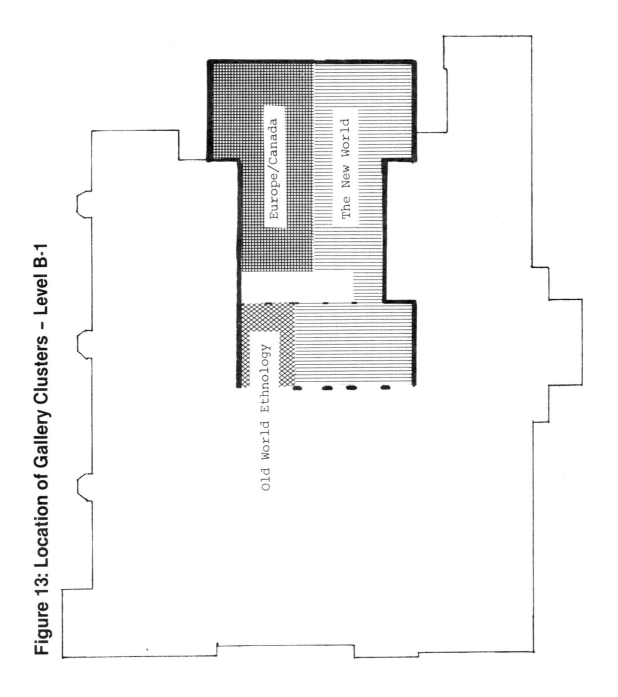

Figure 13: Location of Gallery Clusters – Level B-1

Europe/Canada

The New World

Old World Ethnology

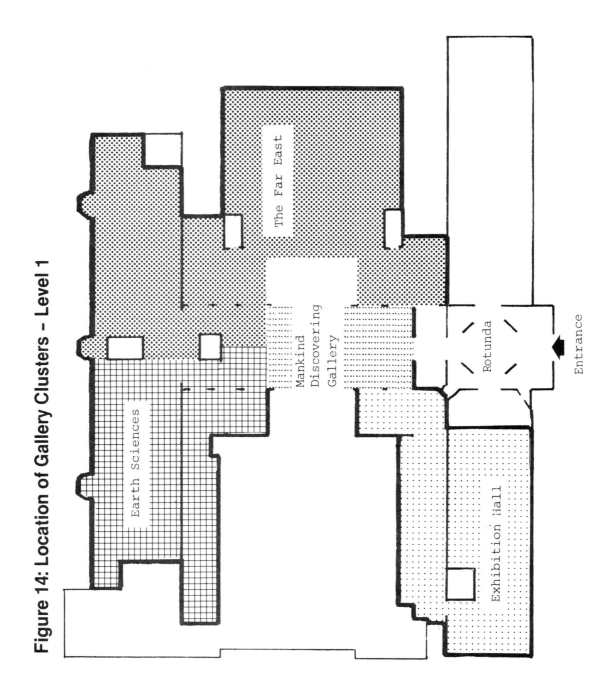

Figure 14: Location of Gallery Clusters – Level 1

The Far East

Earth Sciences

Mankind Discovering Gallery

Rotunda

Entrance

Exhibition Hall

77

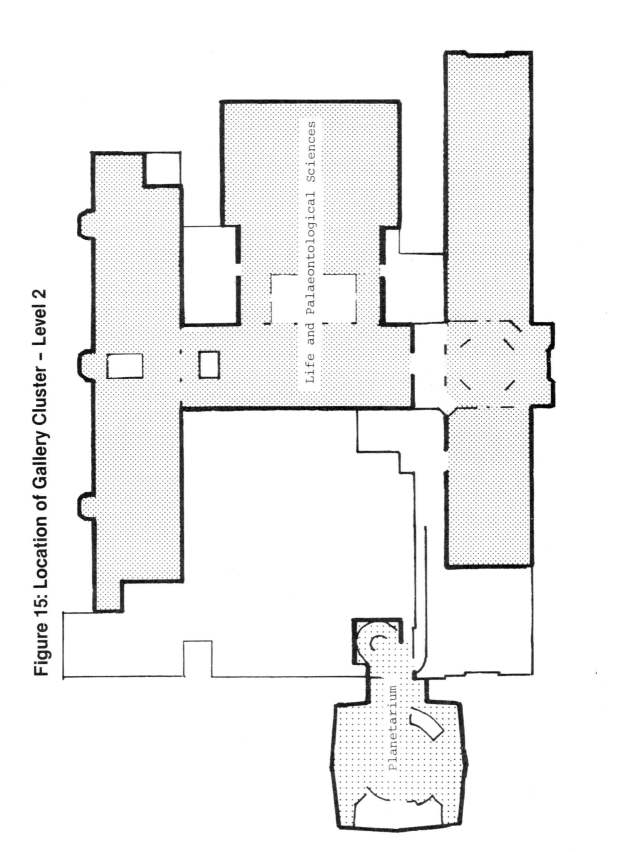

Figure 15: Location of Gallery Cluster – Level 2

Life and Palaeontological Sciences

Planetarium

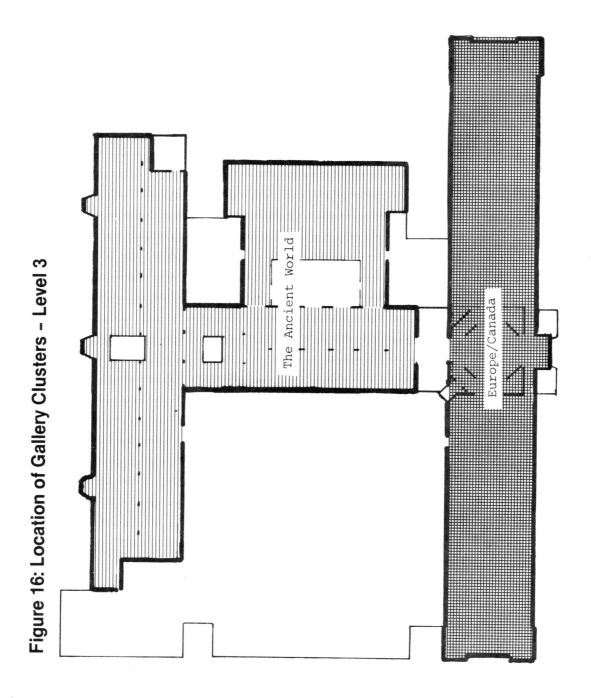

Figure 16: Location of Gallery Clusters – Level 3

The Ancient World

Europe/Canada

B. The Clusters

Descriptions of each of the clusters and special gallery areas follow. They include: communication objectives which express the main ideas in these areas; plans indicating how the gallery space will be used; preliminary allocations of space to individual galleries.

Neither the communication objectives nor the detailed plans are final. As gallery ideas are further developed, both the objectives and the detailed plans will likely evolve.

1. DISCOVERY ROOM

An experimental "Discovery Room" designed at the ROM was very successful with the public. A new discovery room is part of the overall plan and there will be a special facility for preschoolers.

The communication objective for the room is outlined below:

Overall Communication Objective

To provide the public with "discovery" learning opportunities which stimulate interest in the Musuem's collections.

The primary purpose is to provide the visitor with a discovery approach to learning. The secondary purpose is to illustrate the diversity of creations.

The room will present an informal display of study materials which will invite examination and inquiry. It should be designed for easy access and for comfortable use.

The room will contain a variety of collections and will include identification units with collections of natural science and history materials, boxes for discovery learning, and objects for handling and study. Its contents should reflect the wide range of ROM interests and activities.

In order to provide a satisfying discovery experience for preschoolers, a separate "participation" room will be built. It will meet the special physical and mental requirements of these children. A colourful and simple presentation of ideas should encourage a discovery learning experience. The area will be uncluttered, with no fixed displays, so that children can move about freely.

Figure 17: Discovery Room

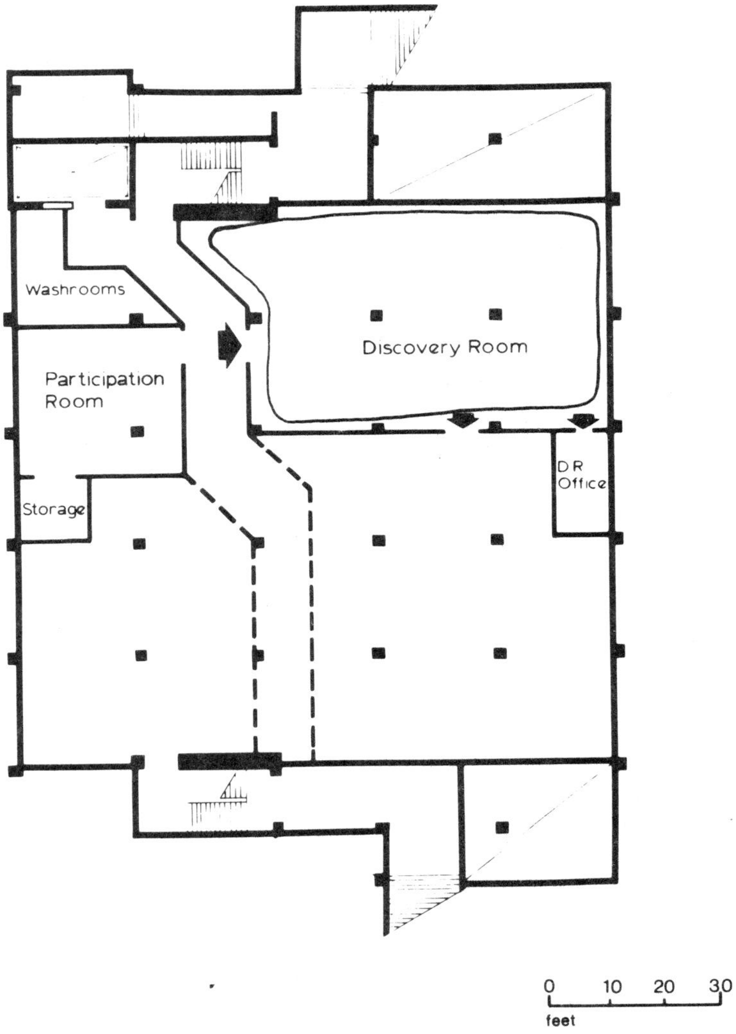

Washrooms

Participation
Room

Storage

Discovery Room

D R
Office

0   10   20   30
feet

Discovery Room

	Sq. Ft.	Sq. Ft.
Discovery Room	2780	
Discovery Office and Work Area	200	
Total		2980

Participation Room
   (Area not included in direct
   allocations to galleries.)

Grand Total	2980

2. EUROPE / CANADA CLUSTER

The Europe/Canada cluster contains the galleries of three departments: European, Canadiana, and Textiles. The galleries of this cluster are divided between two floors, B1 and the third floor. The cluster deals with selected aspects of Western Civilization from Mediaeval times to the present.

Certain special categories of European materials will be located on level B1.

There will also be two Canadiana galleries, the Treasures of Canada gallery and the Environmental gallery (Man versus the Climate), both on level B1. The majority of the Canadiana galleries will remain in the Canadiana Building at 14 Queen's Park Crescent.

Textile galleries will contain frequently changing exhibitions partly to meet the conservation requirements of fragile textiles. Other components of these galleries will have more permanent installations.

The English and Continental collections of the European Department will be organized separately along chronological lines on the third floor.

Special collections, such as European Arms and Armour, the Lee Collection, and the costumes, will also be located on the third floor.

B1 Level: Orientation Statement

The B1 level will house three groups of galleries for the Europe/Canada cluster. Of these, the Canadiana galleries and the Textile gallery will have some conceptual links to the New World galleries on the same level. Certain special collections of the European Department will also be on this level.

Costume and Weaving Technology Gallery

Communication Objectives

*To demonstrate principles of textile and costume production, and
specifically to show fibres, fibre preparation, textile construction,
applied decoration, and garment construction.*

*To serve as a "visual vocabulary" of the textile terminology used through-
out the building.*

The gallery will show how textiles and costumes are made, from
what kinds of raw materials, by what processes, and by what
types of equipment.

European Graphic Arts

Communication Objective

*To present material which has a common denominator in its graphic and
production techniques.*

Since the print collection is large it will have to be presented on a rotating basis, each display relating to a particular theme, country, or period. The stamp collection will
be brought into this gallery, since stamps relate to print
materials and techniques.

European Timepieces and Vertu

Communication Objective

*To exhibit in one gallery the curious hybrid of technology and applied
art seen in the timepiece and its development, together with objects
de vertu, which are often related in style, material, and technique.*

One section of the gallery will be devoted to clocks,
illustrating their stylistic affiliation with furniture.
The presentation of watches will show their distinctive
technological and stylistic development.

Musical Instruments

Communication Objectives

To present a comprehensive display of the history and development of musical instruments, and to illustrate their gradual progress in sound quality, material structure, shape, and decoration.

To explain the use of different instruments in different periods of musical history, and to show musical styles, musical literature, arts, and crafts. To complement the display with a collection of autograph letters and documents of famous musical personalities, and rare music scores and books.

The gallery will contain about 120 musical instruments grouped according to the conventional typological distinctions. There will also be about the same number of autograph letters and rare music scores and books.

Treasures of Canada Gallery

Communication Objective

To present Canadian historical objects of such quality or importance as to be considered national treasures.

This gallery will be object-oriented, with the deliberate goal of drawing attention to particular items rather than to an overall theme or objective.

Canadian Environment Gallery: (Man versus the Climate)

Communication Objective

To discuss the influence of climatic imperatives on Canadian architecture, clothing, food, and occupations.

This gallery will be interdisciplinary, drawing upon materials from the Textile, Botany, Mammalogy, Ichthyology, and the Ethnology Departments.

Figure 18: Europe/Canada Cluster – Level B1

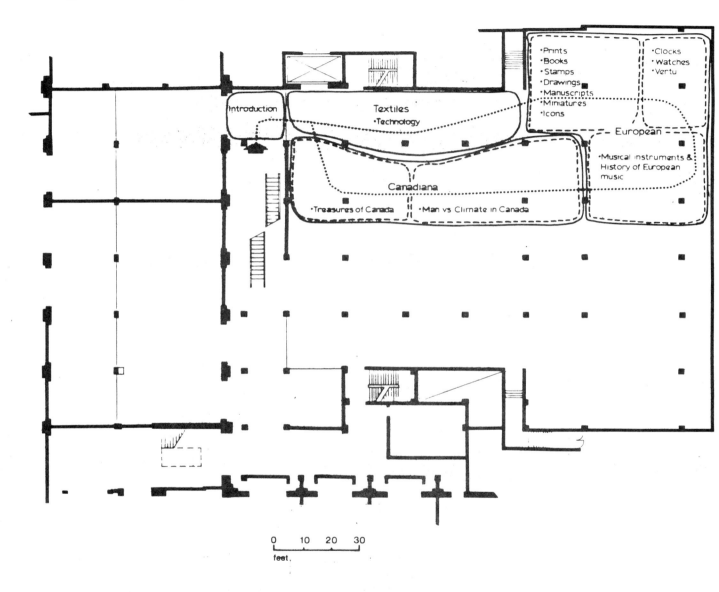

Introduction

Textiles
•Technology

•Prints
•Books
•Stamps
•Drawings
•Manuscripts
•Miniatures
•Icons

•Clocks
•Watches
•Vertu

European

Canadiana

•Treasures of Canada   •Man vs Climate in Canada

•Musical instruments &
History of European
music

0   10   20   30
feet.

Europe/Canada

	Sq. Ft.	Sq. Ft.
B1 Level		
Introduction	400	
		400
Textiles		
Costume and Weaving Technology	1500	
		1500
Canadiana		
Treasures of Canada	1450	
Canadian Environments Gallery	1950	
		3400
European Special Collections		
European Graphic Arts	1500	
European Timepieces and Vertu	800	
Musical Instruments	1700	
		4000

Grand Total   9300

3.   THE NEW WORLD CLUSTER

The New World Cluster of galleries consists of all the New
World Archaeology galleries, a number of Ethnology galleries,
and a common short-term gallery.

The two departments involved have agreed to provide a common
introduction to the galleries of the New World and to arrange
their galleries according to the following geographic divisions:

- Canadian Archaeology and Ethnology galleries

- Other North American Ethnology galleries

- Mesoamerican Archaeology and Ethnology galleries

- South American Archaeology and Ethnology galleries

Some exchange of materials between the two departments is expected, in order to create more comprehensive displays. There
is also interest in creating links between two of the New World
galleries, Ontario Archaeology and the Plains Indians gallery,
and the adjacent Canadiana galleries.

In the following outline of communication objectives, the
individual galleries are grouped according to the main
geographical divisions and are placed in the order in which
a visitor would encounter them if he were to follow the route
through the galleries.

Overall Communication Objective

*To give the visitor an appreciation of New World prehistory and to allow
the visitor to compare ancient and living civilizations of North, Central,
and South America.*

The main circulation pattern will lead the visitor to an introduction to the peopling of the New World. The visitor will
then travel through exhibits of Canadian cultural groups,
through a short-term gallery, to galleries about other North,
Central, and South American cultures.

Introduction (Beringia: The Peopling of the New World)

Communication Objective

To show the geographic proximity of Siberia and Alaska and to indicate possible migration routes across the Bering Straits from the Old World to the New World.

This gallery will tell the history of mankind's first step on the American continent. At the same time the migration of plants and animals will be described. Further, man's dispersal throughout the New World in remote prehistoric times will be shown.

Maps will indicate the land bridges that possibly existed in the Bering Strait area during the last ice age. The same maps will also trace the movement of early people into Canada and the rest of the Americas.

Lithic artifacts will be the principal objects of display, supplemented by graphics of hunting scenes.

Ontario Archaeology Gallery

Communication Objective

To display the prehistory and early history of the Native peoples of Ontario and, to a lesser extent, the early history of the Europeans with whom they were in contact.

The material will be organized both chronologically and culturally. Artifacts, plans, and other archaeological data, reconstructions, maps, etc., will illustrate the material culture, way of life, and environmental context of prehistoric and early historic peoples. If possible, full size dioramas for each of the four major time periods will be incorporated, depicting archaeological as well as ethnographic material.

<u>Woodlands Indians Gallery</u>

<u>Plains Indians Gallery</u>

<u>Northwest Coast Indians Gallery</u>

<u>Subarctic Indians Gallery</u>

<u>Inuit Gallery</u>

<u>Other North American Indians Gallery</u>

<u>*Communication Objective*</u> *(for all galleries listed above)*

To present selected aspects of the interactions of a culture with the natural and social environment.

These galleries will provide analytical presentations based on categories such as the following:

- Painting and pictorial art
- Musical instruments
- Clothing and costumes (e.g., buffalo robes)
- The home (for Inuit gallery, perhaps laid out as an igloo)
- Warfare
- Economy (for Subarctic gallery, a display on trapping)
- Transportation (for Woodlands gallery, display of birchbark canoes)
- Tribute and ceremonial artifacts
- Votive artifacts
- Pipes, smoking, and tobacco
- Panorama case

Mesoamerican Gallery

Communication Objective

To provide the visitor with a general outline of the prehistory of Mesoamerica, with emphasis on the Valley of Mexico and immediately neighbouring areas, as well as the Oaxaca Valley.

The primary purpose of the gallery is to communicate as much as possible of the course of development in Mesoamerica big game hunting to sedentary, agricultural civilizations. In particular, the shifts that marked the emergence of the Post-Classic, with its emphasis on militarism and, in the later centuries of the period, on a tribute-supported central power, should be stressed. Here, as in the Maya display, it is desirable to emphasize both the parallels and the differences between Mesoamerican cultures and our own.

Organization will thus be regional and chronological, with the Valley of Mexico, the region most broadly represented in the Museum's holdings, providing a core exhibit to which smaller holdings from other areas can be related. This presentation will have the advantage of leaving to the last the Oaxaca material, which is the most striking, and which is also geographically closest to the Maya area, coverage of which will be provided in the Maya gallery.

Maya Gallery

Communication Objectives

To provide the visitor with the opportunity to view in detail the development of one society within the Mesoamerican context, and to show how the Museum's work has revealed considerable new information about that society.

One of the subsidiary purposes of the gallery will be to instruct the viewer in some aspects of excavation and of the interpretation of excavated data on Maya sites. In addition, a few glimpses of modern Maya life, illustrating its relation to ancient patterns, will be provided. The gallery will present, without an extensive use of text, enough about the processes involved in the rise and fall of Maya civilization to make viewers think about their own society and the impermanence of all social systems.

The viewers will be led first through a chronological coverage of the ancient Maya, spanning the period from about 1500 B.C. to the 17th century A.D., with emphasis on the Central Lowlands, the area of the Museum's research activities. Contributions made by the Museum's excavations to our understanding of events throughout the time span will be made evident through artifacts and supporting materials, but the principal focus will be on the Maya as a whole, rather than on the Museum's work in particular. After the chronological coverage, viewers will see such things as a replica of a priestly tomb from Altun Ha (or possibly, Lamanai) models of individual structures or portions of the sites excavated by the ROM, and some special objects (of which the large jade head of the Maya sun god is the prime example), which can be appreciated for their aesthetic qualities alone, but will also fit within the framework laid out in the first part of the gallery.

Mesoamerican Ethnology Gallery

Communication Objective

To present selected aspects of the interactions of the cultures with the natural and social environment.

This gallery will provide analytical presentations based on categories such as the following:

- Painting and pictorial art
- Musical instruments
- Clothing and costumes
- The home
- Warfare
- Economy
- Transportation
- Tribute and ceremonial artifacts
- Votive artifacts
- Pipes, smoking, and tobacco
- Panorama case

South American Archaeology Gallery (Peru)

Communication Objective

To give the public an overview of some of the major cultural periods in Peruvian prehistory and an appreciation of the accomplishments of the ancient Peruvians and the distinctiveness of their culture.

The Museum has a small collection of Peruvian material. However, it reflects only three of the four major archaeological periods in Peruvian prehistory (Nazca, Mochica, Chimu, and Inca), with a few pieces from other periods. It is therefore not comprehensive, nor is it particularly representative of Peruvian history as a whole. Although the collection is completely undocumented, most of the materials can be ascribed to particular periods on the basis of style and design.

South American Ethnology Gallery

Communication Objective

To present selected aspects of the interactions of the native South American cultures with the natural and social environment.

This gallery will provide analytical presentations based on categories such as the following:

- Paintings and pictorial art
- Musical instruments
- Clothing and costumes
- The home
- Warfare
- Economy
- Transportation
- Tribute and ceremonial artifacts
- Votive artifacts
- Pipes, smoking, and tobacco
- Panorama case

Figure 19: New World Cluster – Level B1

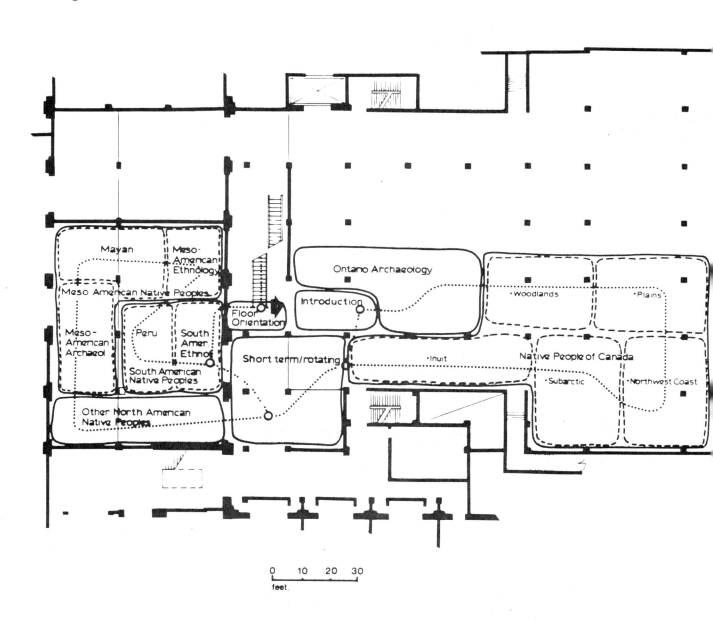

Mayan

Meso-American Ethnology

Meso American Native Peoples

Meso-American Archaeol

Peru

South Amer. Ethnol

South American Native Peoples

Floor Orientation

Other North American Native Peoples

Short term/rotating

Ontario Archaeology

Introduction

Woodlands

Plains

Inuit

Native People of Canada

Subarctic

Northwest Coast

0   10   20   30

feet.

The New World

	Sq. Ft.	Sq. Ft.
Introduction	450	
Short-term Temporary	1680	
Total		2130

Native People of Canada

Ontario Archaeology	1500	
Woodlands (Ethnology)		
Plains (Ethnology)		
Northwest Coast (Ethnology)	6620	
Subarctic (Ethnology)		
Inuit (Ethnology)		
Total		8120

Other North American Native

Peoples (Ethnology)	1150	
		1150

Mesoamerican Native People

Mesoamerican General (Archaeology)	1000	
Maya (Archaeology)	900	
Mesoamerican (Ethnology)	600	
Total		2500

South American Native Peoples

Peru (Archaeology)	500	
South American (Ethnology)	600	
		1100

Grand Total		15000

4. OLD WORLD ETHNOLOGY GALLERY

The Old World Ethnology gallery is an independent (non-cluster) gallery located on B1, adjacent to but separate from the New World Ethnology galleries.

The Old World Ethnology gallery will show cultural manifestations of non-industrial civilizations of the Old World (Africa, Asia, Oceania, Australia). Should further subdivisions of the gallery be required, thematic approaches will provide common denominators for the viewer.

Old World Ethnology

	Sq. Ft.
Old World Ethnology	2750
Grand Total	2750

5. MANKING DISCOVERING: THE THEME GALLERY

The Manking Discovering gallery is Museum-wide in scope, drawing contributions from all departments. It will illustrate the Museum's theme and introduce its galleries.

The following description is the product of a special working group established to define the communication objectives for this gallery. These are stated in some detail in order to define as clearly as possible the gallery's unique role

PREAMBLE

The Mankind Discovering gallery is to be situated directly behind the Rotunda. Because it will be the visitor's first point of contact with the content and messages of ROM, the gallery must not only serve several mechanical functions but must also fulfil its intellectual objectives. It must have ample room for traffic flow because it provides access to the escalators. If this continuous movement is channelled through one section, messages in that area must be comprehensible at first glance. More detailed treatments of subject matter can be handled in less busy areas of the gallery.

The Rotunda should orient the visitor and acquaint him with ROM's physical layout. A large map of the building is suggested for the walls facing the visitor as he approaches the security line. In the Mankind Discovering area, the links between the various disciplines - and hence between the galleries - will be illustrated. The area will also indicate which galleries the individual can visit for more information about any specific subject.

There are a number of requirements that must be clearly recognized before designing begins:

(1) Physically, the ROM is constituted of people, artifacts, and specimens housed in a building. Therefore the displays in the theme gallery should stress this combination through the interaction of people with the objects on display.

(2) The gallery should try to catch the visitor's interest first and foremost. It must be informative without becoming pedantic or boring.

(3)   The visitor must not be burdened with or confused by too
        many ideas or messages in this first gallery. Three pre-
        cepts should be followed to avoid this problem: (a) say
        only a limited amount; (b) state the messages at different
        levels of comprehension so that, regardless of submessages,
        each visitor will grasp the main ones; (c) have some of the
        submessages illustrated by temporary displays.

(4)   Although the gallery should be "permanent", it should be
        possible to replace whole sections from time to time. This
        would allow for the expression of fresh ideas and for the
        adoption of new display approaches while preserving the
        basic message of the gallery.

(5)   Novel contextual relationships (illuminating paradoxes)
        should be used to "startle" a viewer into understanding.

Communication Objectives of Mankind Discovering Gallery

*To illustrate how the Royal Ontario Museum plays a creative role in man's
efforts to discover himself and his universe.*

Throughout recorded history and undoubtedly before, man has
asked: "Who am I, and what am I doing here?" He tries to give
meaning to or find meaning in his existence and that of the universe.

The stated objective embodies ROM's adopted theme. As a means
to achieving this objective, some of the discoveries about man
and his universe will be highlighted in the gallery, but the
visitor must look elsewhere in the Museum for evidence and discoveries to answer many of his questions.

The ROM must recognize that some of these discoveries will not
accord with everyone's beliefs, that some do not show man in a
favourable light, and that some portend a gloomy future for the
human race. Others, however, will support the belief in man's
essential goodness and his high hopes. Thus, the gallery will
be highly thought-provoking and probably controversial, and at
the same time should evoke an emotional response from the viewer.

The objective could be approached in many ways. We recommend
that the gallery should ask, and partially answer, four questions:

(i)   What is a museum? What is the ROM? How does the ROM fit
        into the history of museums? What is the future for
        museums and for the ROM?

(ii)   How do man and nature interact? Does man really have
        dominion over nature? What is the future of man from
        both a biological and philosophical viewpoint? Are there
        real parallels between biological and cultural evolution?

(iii)   What is my place in the world? How do my culture, my
        tradition, my sense of moral value, my judgment of beauty,
        and my ideas of reality compare with those of other cul-
        tures and times? (Man's search for the absolute.)

(iv)   The process of discovering (called research today) - what
        is it? What is its origin and history? What are its
        assumptions and methods?

CONCEPTUAL SUGGESTIONS FOR EACH OBJECTIVE

(i) What Is the ROM?

- Museums are not a recent development; there are many examples
  of ancient museums and zoos. What were the reasons for museums
  in the past and what are they now? Collecting has always been
  a status symbol. We suggest that the Renaissance curiosity
  cabinet, the Oriental museums, and Islamic zoos be used as
  illustrations. Collecting demonstrates an interest in and
  sometimes a veneration for the past. Consequently, mystical
  significance is often ascribed to relics. We recommend the
  juxtaposition of examples: the modern kitchen in which the
  housewife displays old utensils or pots, and the armour and
  weaponry of the ancient warrior into which he incorporated
  the relics of his (or his enemies') ancestors. Collecting is
  often simple avaricious speculation. Examples of real and
  fake artifacts might be used to show this.

- The ROM has a particular role to play in the history of
  museums. What was ROM's history? What is its future? A
  permanent display on the subject is recommended.

- Governments often use museums as a method of preserving
  national treasures and as a focus for patriotism. This can
  easily be shown as part of the ROM's role.

Table III: Mankind Discovering Gallery: Communication Objectives

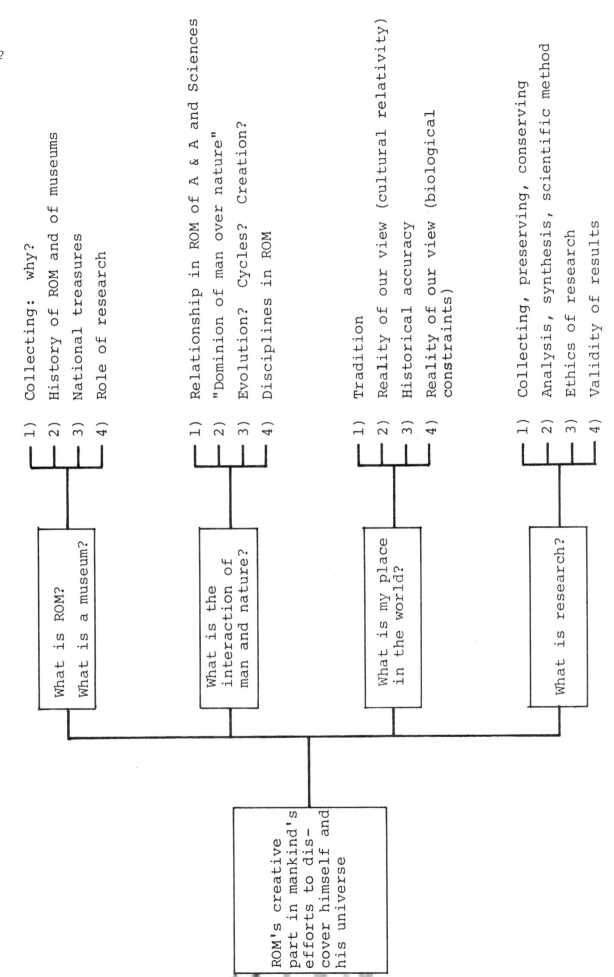

● From these collections the questions arises, "What does this object tell me?" Research has become a major function of museums with extensive collections.

(ii) Interaction of Man and Nature

In this area, ROM needs to demonstrate the bridge between man, his culture and philosophy, and the universe in which he exists and from which he arose.

● Why does one museum (like ROM) house both man-made artifacts and natural specimens? For one thing, it makes an impressive display; for another, it is cheaper to house two collections under one roof - a consideration likely to appeal to civic leaders. But the main advantage of this circumstance is that it makes interdisciplinary approaches possible. We recommend a variety of ways in which to show the symbiotic nature of the relationship. Conservation is a magnificent example and can be exploited for display. Scientific technology in approaching art history problems (X-rays of paintings), sorting out fakes, ageing of artifacts etc., are all relevant possibilities.

● Does man have dominion over nature? Early man developed his own technological methods. He rarely knew why they worked or what their consequences might be. He thought he was taming the forces of nature. Today, man's technology has expanded immensely in accordance with his knowledge. He can predict possible new technologies and also the consequences of existing ones. This display could be composed of two elements: first, an historical sketch which would chart man's technological advances through the ages by examining one or two basic discoveries and tracing their development into the world of today and on into the future; secondly, a question - What will be the cumulative effects of these technologies? (E.g., the development of the use of the wheel or of fire has had many ramifications; the petro-chemically-based land and air vehicle industry; CO_2 in the atmosphere increasing now to "dangerous" levels; mercury in aquatic animals; the commitment to electric power generated by fossil or nuclear fuels.)

● What is the origin of the universe? Evolution? Cycles? Creation? Planetarium participation would be needed with an audio-visual input (including meteors or moonrocks) to convey this message. Because evolution is to be treated in two other galleries, no detailed exposition is necessary, but a specimen display of the development of modern life-forms

(including man) from their origins would introduce the subject. Biological evolution (the progressive change from one
form to another, the result of "inventions" of their ancestors,
which came about in response to selection pressures and
passed into the variable pool of inheritable characteristics)
could be compared to the changes in culture from one period
to another. Does cultural evolution occur? If so, we can
compare its rate of change to that of biological evolution.
Is it a series of destructive cycles in which the inventions of ancestors die following the birth and flowering of
a civilization? In this section there is no fixed answer.
At the boundary between cultural and biological evolution we
can entertain the question of special creation and explore
briefly the issues it raises.

- At this point, an introductory statement could be made about
  the essential make-up of the ROM, its past and its disciplines,
  the operation of its parts, and their location in the building.

(iii)   What Is My Place in the World?

- For intellectual survival, man must find a place for himself
  in the universe, and so he structures his immediate world.
  To overcome his individual frailty, he builds on his ties to
  the past. What are the ways of preserving tradition? Ethnological and archaeological evidence might partly answer this
  question. What is the nature of cultural memory? An example
  could be drawn from the Maya civilization. What are the possibilities of fusing different cultures into new hybrids? Examine the history of Europe in Africa, the future of the South
  Pacific, the spectacular example of the Tasaday's Stone-Age
  culture surviving into the 20th century and the ethics of our
  disturbing it. What role does modern society play in ex-
  ploiting south America, and what is the fate of its many
  Indians?

- We tend to regard our view of the universe and the world
  around us as "correct" and "real". Is it any more real than
  the worlds and universes of other cultures? Contrast the
  ancients' views of the cosmos (mystical, magical) with our own
  (computerized, stark). We can compare our idea of beauty to
  that of other cultures, modern and ancient, by examining the
  nature of art (statuary, the use of colours, or music).

- What is useful? How do ideas of usefulness become involved
  with artistic or decorative concerns? Comparisons of kitchen

ware, cooking utensils, bathrooms, or clothing in different
cultures will demonstrate man's ingenuity in solving problems
and his concern with the aesthetics of each solution. ("Startle"
concepts would work here, e.g., oriental chopsticks in a Western
kitchen table setting.)

A biological parallel becomes evident here. What are nature's
solutions to a given problem? For example, how have various
life forms solved the problem of locomotion through water?
Has man added any solutions? Has nature been "aesthetic" in
her solutions? How do we differentiate between the elegance
of a natural solution and the elegance of a man-made solution?
Is beauty unique to man's consciousness?

● How accurate can our comparisons be? How well do we understand
human history, our own or other people's? The accumulation of
evidence, modern and ancient, often suggests that recorded
history is written to suit the desires of rulers rather than
to reflect reality. A display of examples of the blatant
falsification of history (modern and ancient) should be
assembled. The role of symbolism in prehistory is important.
Can we correctly interpret it today, lacking, as we do, an
experience of that actual time?

● What are the constraints of our animal nature? A display
indicating our sensory limits and a comparison with those
of other animals would be impressive. For example, sound:
we hear from 20-40 cycles per second up to 15,000-20,000
cycles per second while other animals emit and sense sounds
up to 200,000 cycles per second. Of the wide range of electromagnetic waves from very short to very long we are sensitive
only to a minute section. Comparisons could be made to the
"reality" of other animals with the use of filters of heat-
sensitive films, or by simulated hearing through other animals'
brain-ear connections. Finally, the senses that other animals
possess but which we do not (e.g., sensitivity to electric
fields, magnetic fields, etc.) could be explored. The gallery
might then conclude by demonstrating our reliance on the sense
of vision.

(iv) What Is Research?

The concept of using collections as research tools should be introduced. Every specimen and artifact can answer an infinite number
of questions if the investigator has the ingenuity and the tools
to pose them in an appropriate form. This idea can be presented
by using an example (such as a diamond) and examining the

ancient, the early historic, the mediaeval, and the modern analytical views.

Building upon the earlier display on motives for and attitudes
to collecting, a history of the methodology of collecting in
various disciplines could be depicted. This important display
would emphasize the purpose of collecting to preserve as much
information as possible in a given field; comparisons could be
made to art auction purchases or scientific specimen donations.
Another display, on preservation techniques, would stress the
importance of maintaining the integrity of the original material.
Contributions from conservators on the problems of conservation
as opposed to restoration and the dangers to research inherent
in overzealous restoring are recommended here. A comparison can
be made of the different market values of restored and conserved
pieces.

- Analysis, synthesis, the scientific method, logic, and
  serendipity - all are elements of research. Using objects
  drawn from a variety of fields, it should be possible to
  show the viewer the process of analyzing the data available,
  synthesizing the results, and creating an hypothesis. The
  hypothesis would then be tested. The viewer should thus come
  to understand the logic of the process and the validity or
  otherwise of his own logic. The role of serendipity in scientific discovery should be acknowledged, and the personal
  biases and inadequacies of the human observer made clear.
  This display would require audio-visual elements (including,
  possibly, a computer with a pre-programmed package) in order
  to lead the viewer through the complete process of discovery
  and to introduce him to research technology. It is specifically recommended that this display deal with examples taken
  from art history, archaeology, life science, earth sciences,
  and astronomy. Thus, differences in the approaches of various
  disciplines could be illustrated and comments made on their
  varying levels of advancement of knowledge.

- In the course of research, the investigator is forever faced
  with the question of the ethics of his study. Although there
  are no simple answers, a section should be devoted to such
  questions as: Is it moral or ethical in today's world to
  carry out experiments on animals? On humans? Is it wise to
  study evolution and genetics knowing that ultimately genetic
  engineering will allow the shaping of man's anatomy and
  physiology? Is it ethical to study cultural evolution when
  it involves collecting the national treasures of other countries? Do we know enough to make it worthwhile to disturb an
  archaeological site, thus forever destroying the possibility

of studying it again? When does a buried person become an archaeological find?

● What do scientific results mean? Ptolemy's view of the universe was scientifically valid for centuries. How much more correct or incorrect is our own view of the universe? Concepts of atoms and the nuclear processes are now familiar to us, but fifteen years ago the subnuclear particles were theories. Today we reconstruct the evolution of a family of plants; tomorrow, a new technique may prove us completely wrong. How can this be? What is the nature of scientific prediction? Do we really *know* anything?

Figure 21: Mankind Discovering Gallery

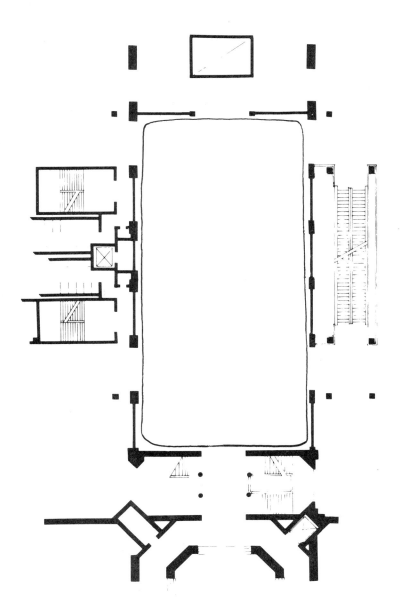

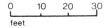

Mankind Discovering Gallery

	Sq. Ft.
Mankind Discovering Gallery	7500

| Grand Total | 7500 |

6. EXHIBITION HALL

Exhibition Hall is the main Museum-wide gallery for temporary
exhibitions. It will accommodate both the ROM's own temporary
exhibitions and travelling exhibitions from outside the Museum.

The additional smaller, temporary exhibition areas in each
cluster are included in the descriptions of individual clusters.

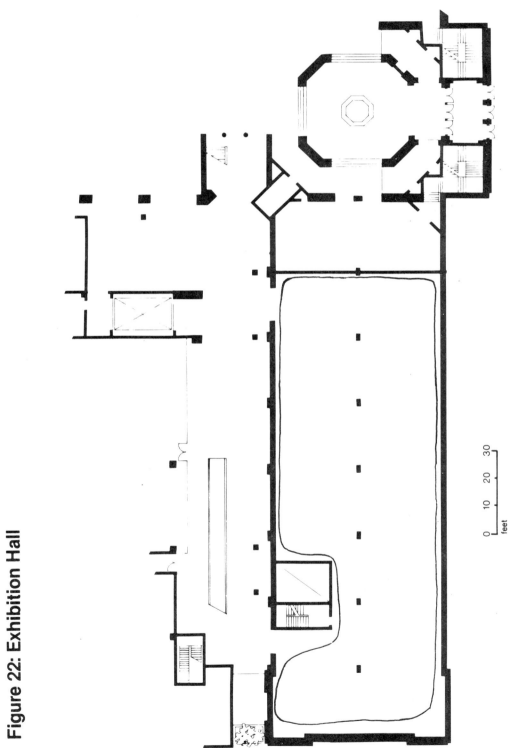

Figure 22: Exhibition Hall

0 10 20 30
feet

Exhibition Hall

	Sq. Ft.
Exhibition Hall (This area can be subdivided to accommodate two exhibits at the same time.)	9250
Atrium Area	4550
Grand Total	13800

7. THE FAR EAST CLUSTER

The Far East cluster consists of the galleries of the Far Eastern Department and a related Textile gallery. The aim of the Far Eastern galleries is to illustrate the social, artistic, technological, and historical development of the material culture of the civilizations of eastern Asia.

The galleries are organized both chronologically and conceptually and begin with an introductory statement describing their organization. The introductory gallery, presenting the prehistory of eastern Asia, begins a sequence that proceeds chronologically through the history of China to the Qing Dynasty.

Origins

The Origins gallery will cover the following topics: the prehistory of East and Central Asia; the archaeology of prehistoric material cultures; the character of the lands and their peoples; and the beginnings of the Chinese language. This gallery shows the archaeological, anthropological, and epigraphical basis for the study of the formation of the principal East Asian civilizations.

Bronze Age China

The Bronze Age China gallery will include various aspects of life in early China as understood through current archaeology and documentary sources. This gallery presents material in light of our current understanding of the social history of early Chinese dynasties. Developing technologies are represented by bronze castings, which are seen as vehicles for artistic expression.

Imperial China

The Chin and Han Dynasties are the periods of unification of the state and the establishment of Empire. The beginnings of patterns of affluence, the widespread use of iron, the expansion of the Empire, and the beginning of contacts with the West are explored. Major developments in glazed pottery and in pictorial arts are highlighted. A wide variety of materials is used to portray the character of life in Han China.

Life and Death - Tang

The full flowering of the Empire through expansion and contacts with the West is seen in part through funerary sculpture of the period. Life in the Tang capital and court, burial customs, and the development of ceramic technique are among the topics to be dealt with in the gallery. The Six Dynasties and Sui will also be featured.

High-fired Tradition

The ceramic development of the previous gallery is expanded here in the first of a series of galleries exploring the ceramic tradition exclusively. Monochrome stonewares and porcelain through the 14th century, including both the imperial and the popular traditions, are presented in terms of their technology and artistic values.

Ming and Qing Porcelains

This gallery will continue the history of fine porcelain up to the 20th century. Emphasis is placed on the development of monochrome glazes and the techniques of overglaze enamelling and underglaze painting.

In the midst of the chronological sequence, two galleries form cul-de-sacs off the Life and Death - Tang gallery. These are the Textile Department's Asian Life-Styles gallery and the Ming Tomb gallery.

Asian Life-Styles: Herder/Farmer

An interdisciplinary demonstration of the geographic and ethnological differences in Asia is shown here. The historical interaction of peoples of opposing life-styles, which nevertheless co-existed until the industrialization of the 20th century, is illustrated.

The gallery will concentrate on identifying the herder socie-ties of the steppe and the agrarian cultures that developed major urban civilizations on the plains. Habitats and histo-rical and ethnographical textiles and costumes will provide evidence of trade, technology, life-style, and unifying tra-ditions.

Ming Tomb

Monumental Chinese funerary sculpture will illustrate feudal ideas of death.

The Pictorial Arts of the Far East gallery follow the main Chinese sequence.

The Pictorial Arts of the Far East

The development of painting and graphic art in China and Japan is presented here. The philosophical, literary, technical, and decorative forces at work on the development of painting are ex-plored. Woodblock prints are seen as an expression of middle-class values.

Three main concept groups follow the Pictorial Arts of the Far East gallery: India, Buddhism, and the Decorative Arts.

India

Hindu-Brahmanic tradition is depicted as a second major focus of civilization in eastern Asia.

The Buddhist arts of Asia continue themes first presented in the Indian gallery and show the development of Buddhist arts in the Far East and South Asia.

Buddhism

Buddhism is a link between the cultures of South and East Asia.
The wide range of Buddhist artifacts will be examined in their
religious, philosophical, historical, and art historical aspects.

The decorative arts of the Far East presented as a cluster,
elaborate concepts of the interdependence, as well as the
uinqueness, of cultures.

Decorative Arts of Ming and Qing

Basic aesthetic values of the two periods are contrasted.
Stylistic changes and methods of manufacture are stressed. The
role of decorative arts in upper-class life is examined..

Decorative Arts of Japan

This gallery will examine decorative arts and ceramics, par -
ticularly those of the Edo Period. The principal concern of this
gallery is the Japanese interest in form and material.

Decorative Arts of Korea

Korean arts and their relationship to those of China and Japan
are presented.

Furniture

Room settings will portray the structural and decorative values
of Chinese and other Far Eastern furniture. The role of furniture in daily life is emphasized.

Figure 23: Far East Cluster

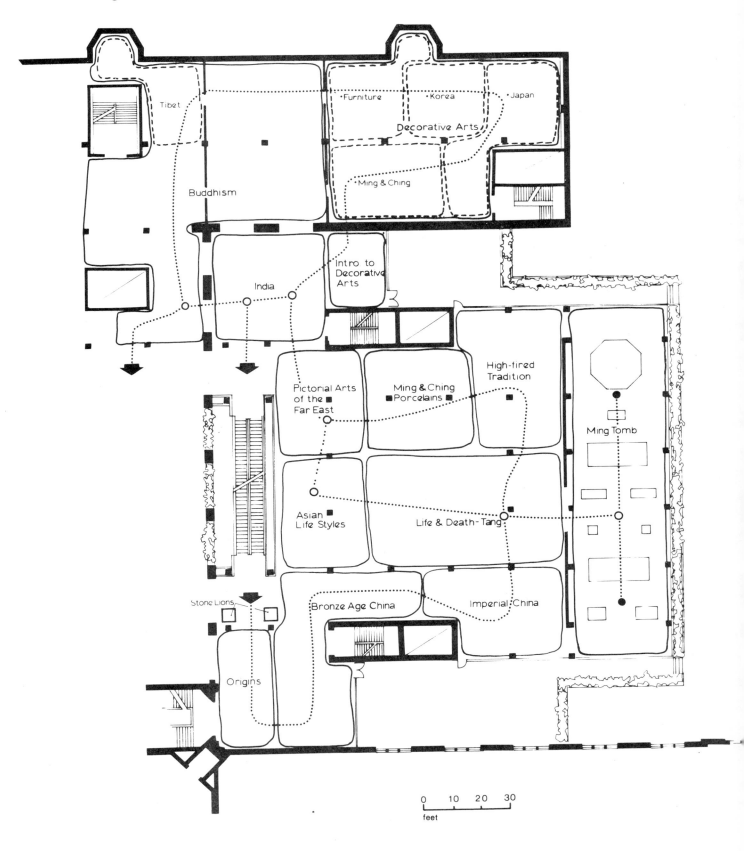

Tibet

Furniture · Korea · Japan

Decorative Arts

Buddhism

· Ming & Ching

Intro to Decorative Arts

India

Pictorial Arts of the Far East

Ming & Ching Porcelains

High-fired Tradition

Ming Tomb

Asian Life Styles

Life & Death-Tang

Stone Lions

Bronze Age China

Imperial China

Origins

0 10 20 30

feet

The Far East

	Sq. Ft.	Sq. Ft.
China		
Origins (Introduction)	900	
Bronze Age China	2200	
Imperial China	1500	
Life and Death - Tang	2800	
High-fired Tradition	1700	
Ming and Qing Porcelains	1500	
Total		10600
Pictorial Arts of the Far East	1200	
		1200
Life Styles (Textiles)	1200	
		1200
India	1700	
		1700
Buddhism	5740	
		5740
The Decorative Arts		
Introduction	600	
Ming and Qing	1200	
Japan	1140	
Korea	1000	
Furniture	1000	
Total		4940
Ming Tomb	4600	
		4600
Grand Total		29980

8.   THE EARTH SCIENCES CLUSTER

The Earth Sciences cluster consists of the galleries of the Mineralogy and Geology Department. Geology and Mineralogy are currently displayed in separate galleries. It is the intention of the department to integrate these two disciplines as fully as possible in its new galleries.

The following is an outline of the communication objectives for the Geology and Mineralogy galleries.

Overall Communication Objective

To educate the public and to give them an appreciation of the sciences of mineralogy and geology.

The major sections of the Geology and Mineralogy galleries, with communication objectives, are outlined below.

Introduction - Geology and Mineralogy

Earth in relation to the Moon, other planets, and the Universe.

Gross Global Structures

Major geological structures and geomorphological features of Earth.

What Is the Crust?

General descriptions of the oceanic and continental crust.

Rocks

Major rock groups that form the crust.

Minerals

Major rock-forming minerals that make up the rocks.

Atoms

Concept of atoms, elements, and compounds.

Teaching Mineralogy

Definition of terms and description of properties of minerals.

Physical Geology

Description of geological processes (mountain building, metamorphism, volcanism, etc.) that shape the Earth's crust, and the classification of rocks.

Stratigraphy

Interpretation of Earth's history.

Geochronology

Absolute (radiometric) chronology and relative chronology of the Earth's crust, and how this is used to correlate rocks of the Earth's crust.

Economic Geology

Man's responsibility to understand and to use knowledgeably the resources of the Earth's crust.

Geochemistry and Mineral Deposits

Geological processes leading to the concentrations of elements that make mineral deposits.

Precambrian Geology

Eighty-five per cent of the Earth's crust, foundations of the continents, world's oldest rocks.

Systematics and Gems

Chemical and crystallographic classification of minerals. Display of the gem collection and some gemmology.

Changing Exhibits

Changing exhibits from either Mineralogy or Geology.

Classic Mineral Occurrences of Ontario and the World

The geology and mineralogy of selected world mineral occurrences. The geology and mineralogy of selected mineral occurrences in Ontario.

Figure 24: Earth Sciences Cluster

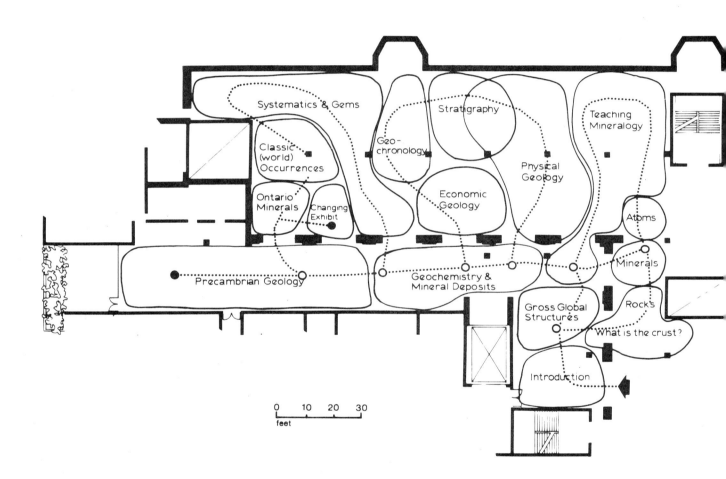

Earth Sciences

	Sq. Ft.
Mineralogy and Geology	15600
Grand Total	15600

9.   THE PLANETARIUM

The main feature of the Planetarium is, of course, the Star Theatre. However, the Planetarium also has a gallery area which will be developed to provide a complementary environment to that of the Star Theatre; to reinforce concepts relevant to Star Theatre programmes, and to present some ideas that are better dealt with in exhibits or mini-theatres.

The following is an outline of the ideas the Planetarium wishes to communicate to the public in this gallery.

Overall Communication Objective

To present through exhibits and other display techniques, concepts on astronomy.

This will include:

- basic astronomical terminology, information and concepts, particularly in the form of visual images, the purpose of which is to enable visitors to connect images to such common terms as Jupiter, star cluster, galaxy.

- astronomical ideas, concepts, and phenomena whose explanation requires a more flexible and participatory learning experience than can be given in the Star Theatre.

- current astronomical and space discoveries.

The Planetarium intends to make extensive use of mini-theatres and other audio-visual techniques in displays.

Because of the area's shape and its dual use (both for display and for access to the theatre), and as a result of unhappy experience with the linear display format, the Planetarium sees the future display as a series of independent areas dealing with a specific topic or related topics. The connecting links will be provided by the overall physical design of the display and by the approach to astronomy and related sciences.

Topic Areas

Topics which might be included in the gallery area are:

- Orientation to the gallery and theatre
- The current night sky
- Earth, moon, and planets
- Exploration of the solar system (mini-theatre)
- Comets
- The Sun
- Stars and stellar systems including star clusters, the Milky Way Galaxy, and galaxies.
- Cosmology and frontiers of astronomy (mini-theatre)
- Cosmic rays and the electromagnetic spectrum
- A children's area of participatory displays
- Current events corner

Other Display Spaces

Though the main circulation path through the Planetarium gallery may not be physically separate from the rest of the display, it should be a clearly defined traffic route. It might also feature space art and astronomical holography. School class exercises could be performed here.

Either the spiral staircase area or the area immediately adjacent must be designed for the assembly of school groups or the queueing of theatre patrons. Thought must be given to visitor comfort and to appropriate decor.

The ramp and atrium area could have two display functions:

(1) to orient the visitor who arrives at the Planetarium by way of the Museum;

(2) to feature hanging displays of rocket and satellite models or other decoration.

Figure 25: Planetarium Gallery

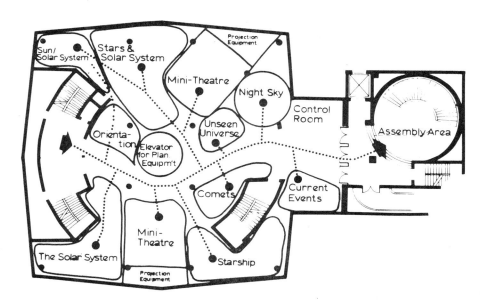

0   10   20   30
feet

Planetarium

	Sq. Ft.	Sq. Ft.
Main Planetarium Galleries	5040	
Total		5040
Circulation and Ancillary Areas		
(Within Main Galleries)	1760	
Total		1760
Other Gallery Areas		
(Beyond Main Galleries)		
Atrium	500	
Assembly Area	200	
Total		700
Grand Total		7500

10.   THE LIFE AND PALAEONTOLOGICAL SCIENCES CLUSTER

This cluster, on the second floor, includes the galleries of the following life and palaeontological sciences departments: Invertebrate Palaeontology, Vertebrate Palaeontology, Botany, Entomology, Invertebrate Zoology, Ornithology, Ichthyology and Herpetology, and Mammalogy.

The Life and Palaeontological Science departments have decided to develop a major integrated gallery to deal with common concerns. In addition, the galleries of the three invertebrate departments will be adjacent to one another and representatives from each are planning to ensure a coherent and logical approach to the history and significance of invertebrates.

It is not yet decided whether the Ichthyology and Herpetology galleries will share the south end of the east wing, or whether the locations of the Ichthyology and Ornithology galleries will be exchanged. The juxtaposition of the Herpetology and Ornithology galleries may affect the communication objectives for both these galleries.

The following outline of life and palaeontological science galleries includes communication objectives for the common Gallery of Life, as well as for departmental galleries, so far as these have been developed to date.

GALLERY OF LIFE

LIFE AND PALAEONTOLOGICAL SCIENCES COMMON GALLERY

Communication Objective

To reveal the sense of order existing within the vast diversity of life that abounds in the world around us, and the basic principles now believed to explain how this diversity evolved.

The Museum is involved in gathering and documenting the evidence upon which our ideas about the basic principles of life are based. Through a process of reconstruction, the scientist reveals order in diversity. Underlying the different ways in which different groups of organisms have solved their common problems, scientists have found basic principles and processes common to the evolution of all life. This gallery describes the history of our knowledge of fundamental bio-logical principles and traces their manifestations in diverse forms of life.

The gallery, which will incorporate as many specimens as possible, will emphasize the processes by which scientists reconstruct order and derive basic themes from the evidence of living and fossil organisms, both plant and animal.

Four main areas will be explored:

(1)   The origin and diversity of life forms, with a statement on the classification of all living things into five kingdoms.

(2)   Our current knowledge of the mechanisms that resulted in the present variety of plants and animals.

(3)   The forces, and the properties of the organisms, that have led to the present diversity of life.

(4)   The biological explanation of the variety of habitats, geographical distribution, and interrelationships of organisms.

Other topics illustrating interdisciplinary themes will be presented, either permanently or temporarily, as the planning process continues.

Individual Communication Objectives

(i) The Origin and Early Evolution of Life

Communication Objectives

To show the earliest and most primitive forms of living matter on this planet, both from the fossil record and as extant organisms.

To describe the conditions under which life could have originated and evolved.

To describe the classification of all living things into five great kingdoms and to discuss schemes of classification.

(ii) History and Principles of Evolution

Communication Objectives

To describe the history of thinking on the subject of biological evolution.

To demonstrate the genetic basis of variation, natural selection, and other similar topics.

(iii) Process of Evolution

Communication Objectives

To describe the factors that influence natural selection.

To illustrate such factors as geographic, temporal, or reproductive isolation which influence speciation and geographical distribution. This section may include an investigation of plate tectonics and similar mechanisms.

(iv) Life Today: The Products of Evolution

Communication Objectives

To examine and to explain biological entities and communities, their geographical distribution and their interrelationships.

To present examples of convergent and divergent evolution, evolution of communities, and other illustrations of the effects of organic evolution operating over long periods of time.

Other topics that may become part of the permanent Gallery of
Life include the following:

- <u>Locomotion</u> - how animals cope with problems of
  moving themselves on land, in air, and in water.
  This could consider skeletal elements, muscles,
  mechanics and energetics, etc.

- <u>Reproduction</u> - illustrated by animals that reproduce by eggs laid either in water or on land,
  and those that reproduce by live birth; further
  illustrated by the different problems and solutions
  encountered in a variety of life forms.

- <u>Energy relationships</u> - the food pyramid, herbivores
  and carnivores, dentitions, digestion, etc.

Several other topics may be added to the permanent section of
the gallery after further planning.

A temporary exhibition area will rotate displays on topics
such as the following:

Integument

Skeleton

Sensory organs and nervous systems

Circulatory systems

Respiration

Hormones

Communication (a large subject with many
                display opportunities)

Migration and navigation

Territoriality

Orientation and habitat selection

Dispersal - plants and animals

Thermoregulation - benefits, mechanisms, etc.

- hibernation and estivation

- hetero and homothermy

- overwintering

Mimicry and protective colouration

Geographic variation

Osmoregulation

Adaptations to hostile environments

Photosynthesis

Genetics - plant

        - animal

Systems of classification

GALLERIES OF VERTEBRATE FOSSILS

Overall Communication Objective

To demonstrate by means of good examples the wide range of knowledge we can gain from the study of vertebrate fossils.

Because much of the present gallery area is occupied by successful large displays (dinosaurs, dioramas, etc.) the proposed changes will be confined largely to the south part of the West Gallery, and the vacated office area at the north end.

(i) Communication Objective

To introduce Vertebrate Palaeontology, with special reference to the kinds of material studied, how fossils are collected, and how they are studied and interpreted.

This will include:

- illustrations by means of genuine material of the different kinds of fossils and fossilization;

- diorama (existing) of the work involved in collecting fossils;

- possibly a mini-theatre to show in more detail the basic structural plan of vertebrates, how they function in various media (land, air, and water), and how their skeletons (with special reference to fossils) reveal much about their mode of life, lines of descent,etc.;

- three-dimensional displays using actual fossil skeletons of some of the above, plus other material on the history of Vertebrate Palaeontology and of the field work involved in collecting vertebrate fossils.

(ii) Communication Objectives

To show the variety and evolutionary progression of fishes throughout geological time; to relate to the kinds of living fishes and to the phyletic line which led to the Amphibia.

To show the success and limitations of the Amphibia, and the subsequent evolution of the Reptilia which depended on the amniote egg, a device which freed the early tetrapods from the dependence on water for repro-duction.

To indicate the tremendous variety of reptiles which exploited land, sea and air, especially in the late Palaeozoic and Mesozoic.

Displays will include:

- a statement on the origin of vertebrates;
- varieties of very ancient jawless fishes (both as real specimens and life restorations);
- examples of the numerous lines of fishes lead-ing (a) to living fish groups and (b) to the first land-dwellers;
- possibly an audio-visual presentation on the water-to-land transition and the significance of the development of the egg;
- skeletons of a diverse variety of amphibians and reptiles, showing their specializations, etc., and their relationships, if any, to living forms.

(iii) Communication Objectives

To show mammals of the Pleistocene, featuring those from Ontario, North America, and South America.

To tell the story of the variety of mammals during the last sixty million years, but most especially the last million or so, with emphasis on the late Pleistocene extinction, transmigration of faunas across the Panamanian isthmus, and evolution of the horse.

Displays will show:

- examples of animals that only recently became extinct, including a mount of mastodon (existing).
- fossil mammals from North and South America (two dioramas, one existing) and the lineal evolution of the horse. The latter should have the aid of audio-visual interpretation.

This section will deal mainly with relatively familiar mammals.

(iv) Communication Objective

To show the variety of life in the sea at the time when the dinosaurs dominated the land. This will use our present "underwater" diorama, and Holzmaden slabs, plus additional material from the epicontinental sea of North America.

Additional specimens will be added to the area adjacent to the present aquatic diorama; this will show material as it is found and will show some specimens which are not yet on display, (e.g., giant fish).

(v) Communication Objective

A temporary exhibit area which will be kept as adaptable as possible. There should be no fixed cases, but adequate space for the display of single large objects or several small display units.

This area will reflect current issues, new acquisitions, research, field work, and newly prepared specimens.

(vi) Communication Objective

To display a wide variety of complete skeletons of Canadian Upper Cretaceous Dinosaurs, along with habitat material and an interpretive audio-visual presentation.

This is the existing Cretaceous Dinosaur Section.

- In the first section, three wall-mounted hadrosaurs against a simulated sandstone background.

- A mini-theatre (rear screen, two-projector slide show) with special emphasis on dinosaurs.

- In the second section a number of skeletons set among simulated natural vegetation appropriate to the Upper Cretaceous, about seventy million years ago.

(vii)   Communication Objective

To present a typical grouping of Jurassic age dinosaurs from Western United States.

This is the existing Jurassic gallery.

(viii)   Communication Objectives

To show how ancient is the line leading to our present day mammals, and to show how the mammals became specialized for different modes of life.

- One of the earliest mammal-like reptile skulls, with a discussion of the difference between a mammal and a reptile. Examples of ancient extinct mammals.

- Several skeletons and skulls of mammals from North America.

- Probably an audio-visual show to explain early mammalian diversity, results of isolation (South America, Australia, etc.), and other mammal stories as we develop the scenario.

(ix) Communication Objectives

To present kinds of dinosaurs not presently on display.

To display specimens which illustrate modern ideas on dinosaur energetics: physiology, locomotion, etc.

To provide a space for temporary displays, especially those dealing with dinosaurs.

To discuss current ideas on relationships between dinosaurs and birds.

Complete and partial skeletons, mostly genuine but with some replicas, will be displayed. Much of the material will be rather spectacular. This area is an expansion and amplification of the current dinosaur display, giving us an opportunity to show more variety and offer more facts and theories about dinosaurs. The arrangement and design will have to be reconciled with the present gallery.

ORNITHOLOGY GALLERIES

Communication Objectives

To provide autodidactic material on the major aspects of avian biology.

To explain evolutionary concepts and controversies with reference to birds.

To show the diversity of bird life in the world and to illustrate the concepts of ecological equivalents, convergence, and parallelism.

To illustrate and assist in the identification of Ontario birds.

To indicate the contribution of Museum research to our general knowledge of the biology of birds.

To illustrate the effects of environmental alteration on bird life in particular and all life in general.

To teach the "why" of bird classification as well as the traditional "how".

The diversity of the collection will be illustrated by the use of dioramas depicting major biomes of the world, e.g., tundra, coniferous forest, deciduous forest, savannah, desert, etc. The department wishes to replace the traditional mounts and cases with interpretative taxidermy depicting birds in real life situations.

The department would like a combination of fixed and temporary displays. The fixed displays would be dioramas as outlined above, and the temporary exhibits would be strategically located in the galleries to present a changing focus at regular intervals. Current research results and various aspects of avian biology such as migration, reproduction, etc., would be suitable for changing displays.

The department would also like to have a large flight cage in the main gallery to emphasize that much of its research is on live birds. Various species of African and Australian parrots are brilliantly plumaged and easy to keep, and perform well in captivity for audiences.

ICHTHYOLOGY AND HERPETOLOGY GALLERIES

Overall Communication Objective

To provide a series of examples of fishes, their several parts, and the principles by which they live and die.

The gallery will provide living examples, mounts, whole pickled specimens, and graphics of local and exotic species. It will define general principles and will show the ROM's participation in discovering those principles. It will provide a macro- and a micro-view of new discoveries made at the cutting edge of science both at the ROM and elsewhere.

Individual Communication Objectives

To provide a view of the world of fishes, stressing the diversity of form, the evolutionary sequence, the ecological interactions between fish, other animals, and the environment.

To indicate the relationship between form and life history as exemplified by both generalized and highly specialized fishes.

To represent a modest array of local species and some indication of their habitat.

To illustrate the departmental research and its relevance both to the people of Ontario and to mankind in general.

To keep people informed of current issues in the field of ichthyology in a way that is interesting and informative.

This will take the form of:

- permanent displays or dioramas, explaining by examples and illustrations the general principles of evolution, life history, etc., as they apply to fishes;

- semi-permanent displays, using the preceding themes and focusing attention on them; e.g., function design (how fish swim), behaviour (how fish communicate), etc;

- temporary displays using "discovering" as a main theme and drawing on recent activities of the department or major recent discoveries by other scientists. News items or historical material will also be used.

INVERTEBRATE GALLERIES

The three departments responsible for living and fossil invertebrate animals, Invertebrate Palaeontology, Invertebrate Zoology, and Entomology, will occupy gallery space adjacent to one another in the second-floor Terrace galleries. While each department will retain galleries with its particular subject matter, representatives of the three departments are planning to confer with each other both before and during the operations of the individual gallery development teams. Their aim will be to ensure that there is no duplication of effort and that a coherent and logical storyline covering the history and significance of invertebrates is presented to the Museum visitor.

INVERTEBRATE FOSSILS GALLERIES

Overall Communication Objectives

To provide an understanding of the vastness of geologic time, of organic evolution over 3.4 billion years, and of the telling of "time" using invertebrate and plant fossils.

To familiarize the public with basic concepts of palaeobotany, palaeoecology, and taxonomy.

To provide encouragement for the collection, conservation, and identification of common local invertebrate fossils.

Three individual galleries with communication objectives are listed below:

Chronologic Gallery

To introduce the concepts and vocabulary of invertebrate palaeontology, including evolutionary change, documented with fossils from our collections.

Thematic Gallery

To provide details of the concepts of the science that have only been touched on, and to expand on the use of fossils to illustrate the mechanisms of evolution, research, and biostratigraphy.

Integrated Gallery

To demonstrate how invertebrate palaeontology and palaeobotany interrelate with other fields such as vertebrate palaeontology, geology, mineralogy, invertebrate zoology, etc.

INVERTEBRATE ZOOLOGY GALLERIES

Overall Communication Objective

To show that every organism is of consequence for the continuity of life. Each organism forms a link in the food chain which maintains life. Animals, irrespective of size or appearance, whether cellular or multicellular, must perform the same basic life activities (ingestion, digestion, secretion, elimination, assimilation, respiration and reproduction). The importance of the individual's life lies in its contribution to the maintenance of life.

Temporary Displays

(1) Topics of current interest: ecological studies, medical research, social research, experimentation in psychology.

(2) Objects on temporary loan from other museums.

(3) Aquarium.

Fixed Displays

(1) Invertebrates from Canadian oceans (marine).

(2) Invertebrates from Ontario (freshwater).

(3) Mechanical principles of invertebrate skeletons.

(4) Organelles and organ systems.

(5) Commercial value of invertebrate animals.

(6) Reasons for differences in shape and size of invertebrate animals.

(7) Invertebrate evolution.

ENTOMOLOGY GALLERIES (ARTHROPODS)

Overall Communication Objectives

To show a small part of the vast diversity of arthropods in general and of insects and arachnids in particular.

To show some of the remarkable things these creatures do.

To give the visitor a glimpse of the richness and complexity of the natural world of which he is a part.

Insects and arachnids comprise more than eighty per cent of all known living animal species. They are important components of most natural communities and are of immense importance in maintaining balanced ecosystems. Collections of the department, supplemented by graphics of various sorts, are well suited to communicating this information.

Individual galleries with communication objectives are listed below:

Introduction to Arthropods

This gallery will introduce the viewer to arthropods.

Definition and examples of five basic groups or classes of arthropods: crustaceans, arachnids, insects, centipedes, millipedes. Statement of biological significance of arthropods as the group to which eighty per cent of all living animal species belong. The gallery will include living examples of arthropods.

Arachnids and Myriapods

This gallery will offer general statements about what arachnids and myriapods are and what roles they fill in natural communities.

Spiders, mites, scorpions, etc., will be treated from the standpoints of systematics and of biology; centipedes and millipedes will be similarly treated.

Crustaceans

This gallery will introduce the viewer to crustaceans.

Groups of crustaceans will be treated from the viewpoint of systematics and biology.

Insects

This gallery will help the viewer to use his own experience with insects to gain a better understanding of the vast diversity and biological importance of these animals.

Insects will be treated from the viewpoint of systematics and biology.

Arthropods and Man

Illustrations will be provided of the ways in which arthropods have a direct bearing on the welfare and interests of man:

e.g., balanced environments; food production through pollination; disease transmission; agricultural and forest damage; biological control; food web interdependence by other organisms' domestic occurrence; human food; religious implications, etc.

This gallery will include an exhibit dealing with methods of collecting and studying various groups of arthropods. The gallery will also include a changing exhibit on various aspects of the work of the Department of Entomology.

Arthropod Reference Collection Gallery

The purpose of this gallery is to display reference collections of insects and other arthropods from Ontario for examination by the general public and by amateur collectors. This gallery will also be equipped as a manned identification centre, and will have reference specimen drawers, microscopes, and table surfaces for supervised use by the public. Such units will be designed specifically for secure storage when the area is not supervised. The area should be so arranged that lectures and gallery talks can be given.

MAMMALOGY GALLERIES

Overall Communication Objectives

To show:

- *the evolution of mammals, their distinctive character-istics, and their relationship to other vertebrates;*

- *general mammalian characteristics and specializations;*

- *mammals and nature; survival, adaptions, ecological niches, and the important role of mammals in ecosystems;*

- *mammals of Ontario; rare and common species, their ecology and distribution;*

- *diversity and zoogeography of mammals - to illustrate the many kinds of mammals and their geographical distribution.*

Mammals are important components of all environments, and they represent some of the smallest and largest living vertebrates. The objectives will be communicated by per-manent dioramas and fixed displays, using mounts now in the galleries, as well as new ones - a minimal number from the collections of the department - and graphics.

The department will emphasize fixed displays, but there will also be temporary exhibits based on current research, and on such aspects of mammalian biology as urban mammals, echolocation, migratory patterns, mammals and public health, and other similar topics.

Three individual galleries with communication objectives are:

Introduction to Mammals

This gallery will illustrate the unique characteristics of mammals, including man, and will show how they differ from other vertebrates. The basic groups or orders of mammals will be defined with examples (dioramas, preserved spec-imens, graphics), and concepts of the evolution of mammals will be presented. Domestication; anatomical and physio-logical adaptations, including locomotor and reproductive specializations; and economic importance will be illustrated by bones, skins, and specimens specially prepared for exhibi-tion purposes, and by graphics.

Ontario Mammals

This gallery will introduce the viewer to the various mammals of the Province, and, by demonstrating their diversity, will also help in identification not only of rarely encountered species, but of common ones such as squirrels, and conspicuous ones such as bear and moose. Mounted specimens and graphics will illustrate the species, the ways in which they adapt to the changing seasons, and their roles in the ecosystem. Nocturnal and diurnal, circadian and circannual adaptations, as well as the effect of alteration of the environment, are some topics to be illustrated in this gallery.

Mammals of the World

This gallery will illustrate the diversity of mammals on a global scale, and also the uniqueness of certain groups, e.g., primates and bats. The concepts of convergence, parallel evolution and ecological equivalents will be illustrated, as well as differences and similarities of the mammalian faunas of the world zoogeographic regions.

BOTANY GALLERIES

Overall Communication Objective

To present botanical themes of plant use, the evolution of organisms and vegetation, and dioramas of particular world floras.

The biological support drawn by the animal kingdom from the planet Earth is almost entirely translated through plant chlorophyll, the generator of primary foods. This food base takes many forms in natural and man-made settings; our knowledge of the evolution of its elements and its assemblages is essential to an understanding of our living environment.

The five individual galleries with communication objectives are listed below:

Flora and Vegetation Gallery (Principles Gallery)

An introduction to general principles of vegetational change, diversity, and organization.

Plants and Man

An introduction to various themes of our cultural relationship with plants.

The Plant Kingdom (Systematics Gallery)

An introduction to the diversity of the world's plant kingdom and how scientists organize it.

Dioramas

The theme of this gallery has not yet been determined. A possible one would be "Extreme Environments" (e.g., dry, tropical, arctic, wet, rocky, cliffside, maritime, acid, etc.).

Current Theme Gallery

A changing exhibit of particular departmental research and display interests.

Life and Palaeontological Sciences

	Sq. Ft.
Common Gallery	7500
Vertebrate Palaeontology	10720
Ornithology	3360 or 2750*
Ichthyology	2750 or 3360*
Herpetology	3360
Invertebrate Galleries**	
Invertebrate Palaeontology	6000
Invertebrate Zoology	1540
Entomology	2900
Botany	2520
Mammalogy	15000
Grand Total	55650

---

*The allocation of space to these two departments will depend upon which variant of the plan is ultimately selected.

**The allocation is considered flexible pending development of the concept and design which may reflect departmental and inter-disciplinary spaces differently.

11.   THE ANCIENT WORLD CLUSTER

The Ancient World cluster, on the third floor, comprises the Greek and Roman, Egyptian, West Asian, and Textile departments. These departments have decided to integrate their messages around a chronological sequence and various common themes.

An outline of the collective communication objectives developed for each time period follows. These objectives will be presented essentially through the display of artifacts.

The plan consists of an introductory gallery followed by galleries grouped according to the following time bands:

(1)   Lower and Middle Palaeolithic Man

(2)   Upper Palaeolithic and Neolithic Man

(3)   Early States

(4)   Emerging Powers

(5)   The Hellenistic Centuries

(6)   Empires in Conflict: Rome and Parthia

(7)   The Growth of Ideologies

These are not titles for galleries but rather descriptions of relationships among galleries, the subject of which will be referred to in the introductory spaces.

Overall Communication Objective

To describe man's experience in the Ancient World, as mirrored in the ROM's collections and research interests.

The purpose of the galleries is to tell the story of man as he emerged in the Ancient World, an area that should be seen as distinct from other cradles of civilizations (the Far East, India, and the New World). The Ancient World was one centre for the development of man the influences of which extended both east and west. The story of Western man can be traced continuously from the Ancient World.

THE ANCIENT WORLD INTRODUCTORY GALLERY

Communication Objectives

To introduce the chronological organization of the galleries of the Ancient World.

To provide a geographical orientation.

A giant three-dimensional model can be used to illustrate geographical regions, cultures, and the time bands around which galleries are being developed. Colour-coding can serve to relate galleries to different geographical areas, but it must not be overdone. For example, colours in signs can indicate the paths that visitors can follow if they wish to trace one culture through the total time period. Lighting could be used in the model to pick out time bands.

The galleries are laid out according to the chronological development of the Ancient World, starting with common aspects of the development of man and then going on to demonstrate the diversity that developed in different geographic areas. The extent of cultural diversity or similarity among cultures throughout the Ancient World varied over time. Themes reflecting this variation (language, religion, technology, etc.) provide threads to run through the galleries and should be introduced at the beginning. Some of these themes might be changed from time to time. Some might also be picked up again in a concluding statement at the end of the chronological flow of galleries, again indicating evidences of continuity and the contributions of the Ancient World to present-day cultures. This would help to provide a link to the adjacent European galleries.

LOWER AND MIDDLE PALAEOLITHIC MAN

Communication Objective

To discuss earliest man in the Ancient World.

This is to be a common gallery for all the departments concerned. The concepts to be discussed are common to all areas
of the Ancient World, although even here there is the beginning of diversity. The story of the physical evolution of man
will introduce the visitor to the Lower Palaeolithic period.
Questions such as "Why did the biological development of man
occur in the Old World?" and "Why did the area flourish?"
should be explored. Worldwide climatic change and its impact
must be discussed in this context. (Subsequent galleries will
deal with local climates.) The development of culture (including language) should be introduced here. In order to counter
the anthropocentric view, it should be stressed that man is
only one element of the environment.

UPPER PALAEOLITHIC AND NEOLITHIC MAN

Communication Objectives

To demonstrate the growing cultural diversity of man in the Ancient World in the Upper Palaeolithic Period.

To trace the history of the discovery and spread of agriculture in the area.

This is a common gallery to which all departments will contribute. The time frame is roughly 35,000 B.C. to (in Europe) as late as 2500 B.C.

This gallery will deal with various forms of cultural diversity caused by and reflected in language, subsistence systems, artistic styles, settlement patterns, and social and political structures.

Rates and kinds of cultural change and adaptation vary considerably throughout the Ancient World and should be emphasized. Neolithic cultures from different areas and different time periods could be juxtaposed by way of illustration.

It will be important to explain the gradual shift in man's subsistence strategies during the Neolithic period from hunting and gathering to agriculture and herding, and the causes and consequences (including the non-economic consequences) of the change. An introduction to textiles (feltmaking was dependent upon the domestication of animals) might be presented here.

Explanations of social developments (e.g., the rise of tribalism) will provide a link with the presentation of social and political organization in the next time band (Early States). One aspect of the Neolithic Revolution could be illustrated by examining briefly some peoples who still maintain Neolithic patterns of life.

EARLY STATES

Communication Objective

To demonstrate diversity in the development of social and political organization within the Ancient World.

The presentation of this time period will begin with a brief common introductory statement, and will then branch into individual galleries for Ancient Mesopotamia (to 2000 B.C.), Central and Atlantic Europe (to 1000 B.C.), followed by Early Egypt (to 2000 B.C.), the Aegean Bronze Age (to 1100 B.C.), and the Levant (to 1200 B.C.).

The common statement should explain why diversity developed. It should be pointed out to the visitor that although from this point on the galleries are organized according to stages of socio-political development, this is only one possible arrangement. Objects which might provide a focal point for a common introductory statement include royal figures, temple models, etc.

At this stage in time there were radical differences throughout the Ancient World, although common themes can be recognized, namely, the development of social and political organizations, religion, and technology. Various sub-themes could also be examined, e.g., writing, economic redistribution and trade, and the availability of raw materials.

Civilizations were beginning to arise, but they were less highly organized than those of the later ages of international powers. These early states were less self-sufficient and more subject to external stimuli.

This band represents the Chalcolithic and Bronze Ages. The continuity from the Neolithic to the Bronze Age should be stressed. Continuity to the present can be illustrated through irrigation and construction techniques.

EMERGING POWERS

Communication Objectives

To show how powers emerge and develop in different parts of the Ancient World.

To describe the interchanges between early empires.

This stage in cultural development will be represented by a set of galleries which may not require any common introductory statement other than a map and a brief comment. The visitor will proceed through the Later Mesopotamia gallery, Middle and New Kingdom Egypt and Egypt Abroad, the Egyptian Religion gallery, and Early Nubia, to classical Greece and Pre-Roman Italy.

The common themes of this stage will be developed within the individual galleries. Both international relationships (trade, war, religion) and the growth and importance of individual cultures should be highlighted. The beginning of rivalry between powers and a concern with what others were doing and with territorial control were now appearing.

This time band relates in part to the Bronze Age, and in part to the beginnings of the Iron Age.

THE HELLENISTIC CENTURIES

Communication Objectives

To demonstrate the effects of the first world empire (Alexander the Great) on the Ancient World as a whole.

To show at the same time the continuation of indigenous traditions.

The Hellenistic centuries will be represented by galleries which deal with native and Hellenizing influences.

The themes in these galleries move from socio-political description to a description of cultural expression. The impact of Hellenism is seen mainly in artifacts of material culture (art and architecture). The Hellenizing influence was a veneer that varied in thickness and expression. In most cases the native and Hellenizing cultures existed side by side. The two formal and official types of art in Egypt, the indigenous and the superimposed Hellenistic Greek, will provide an example.

EMPIRES IN CONFLICT

Communication Objectives

To demonstrate the influence of the Roman Empire in the West.

To trace the emergence of the Parthian Empire astride the trade routes to the East.

This set of galleries will flow directly from the previous time band, beginning with a brief introductory statement to orient the visitor to the idea of two empires in conflict. Galleries representing Imperial Rome and the Roman provinces will follow. The Later Nubian and Egyptian galleries branch off from the Roman galleries and also connect physically to Early Nubia. The last two galleries include the Silk Road, which links Rome to Parthia.

The introductory statement should indicate that the conflict between Rome and Parthia was primarily a struggle over trade routes and territorial expansion. These empires also exerted pressures on and were subject to pressure from peoples living in the peripheral areas, such as Northern Europe, India, and Central Asia. The development of Parthia also marks the beginning of a new Iranian identity.

The gallery will also discuss cultural development in the Roman Empire in the West.

The desire to control areas and resources for commercial and political reasons generated a certain pressure towards uniformity. However, the theme of diversity should not be obscured by too strong an emphasis on the two empires themselves.

THE GROWTH OF IDEOLOGIES

Communication Objectives

To demonstrate the significance of the growth of ideology in the polarization of the area into two camps in the pre-modern period.

To describe the Byzantine and Christian sphere and its co-existence with the Islamic World.

This time band begins with an extensive description of the ideologies by which the new political units were shaped: Judaism, Zoroastrianism, and Christianity, along with Mithraism and other mystery religions. The Judaic tradition, its roots going back to earlier times, played a large role. Only artifacts reflecting ideology will be included.

This religion gallery should stress that this was the time when empires were being formed around ideology and the beginning of a period when both civilizations involved individuals who were deeply religious in their personal lives. Ideology prompted and justified empire-building and affected national political systems. Civilization was becoming more complex.

While the ROM does not have collections from the core of Byzantium, its Coptic and Byzantine textiles and coins, together with material from Egypt and Palestine, can be used to illustrate the life of the Christian community outside the metropolitan centre of the Empire.

The area serves as a bridge to Sassanian Persia, Byzantium, and Islam. Because the latter two co-existed and it is their co-existence that is of particular interest, the visitor will be guided into two different streams, Christian and Muslum.

Considerable space will be needed to encompass the long period of time (over 1,300 years) and the broad geographical area (from Spain to India) over which the highly complex Islamic civilization developed. The Islamic galleries will stress pan-Islamic unity by selecting themes such as urbanism, international trade, pilgrimages, and the idealization of nature, with links back to Sassanian Iran.

A gallery in the form of a linear bazaar, housing artifacts but also serving as a circulation route, will stress the theme of international trade linking Islam with Christian Byzantium and Europe, while at the same time physically demonstrating their separation. From the bazaar, which will emphasize technology

as well as the finished products, galleries will take the
form of a Persian garden with pavilion, a religious shrine,
and an introduction to forms and features of urban settlement (such as the bazaar itself).

A small concluding gallery displaying material from Europe
of the Dark Ages will provide a link between Byzantium and
Mediaeval Europe and will serve as a secondary orientation
point for visitors who go directly to the European galleries,
or who view the Ancient World galleries in reverse.

The Ancient World

	Sq. Ft.	Sq. Ft.
Introduction	1000	
Short-term Temporary	1500	
Lower and Middle Palaeolithic	2100	
Upper Palaeolithic and Neolithic	2100	
Introduction To Early States	400	
Total		7100

Early States

	Sq. Ft.	Sq. Ft.
Ancient Mesopotamia	800	
Central Europe	500	
Atlantic Europe	500	
Early Egypt	1400	
Aegean Bronze Age	1200	
The Levant	700	
Total		5100

Emerging Powers

	Sq. Ft.	Sq. Ft.
Later Mesopotamia	1700	
Middle and New Kingdom, and		
Egypt Abroad	2500	
Religion	1500	
Early Nubia	500	
Classical Greece	3600	
Pre-Roman Italy	750	
Total		10550

Hellenistic Centuries

	Sq. Ft.	Sq. Ft.
Hellenism	750	
Republican Rome	300	
Total		1050

Empires In Conflict

	Sq. Ft.	Sq. Ft.
Rome and The Provinces	4000	
Parthia	500	
Silk Road	500	
Late Nubia	1000	
Late Egypt	400	
Total		6400

The Growth Of Ideologies

	Sq. Ft.	Sq. Ft.
Transitions	1200	
Sassanian Persia	500	
Byzantium	800	
Islam	2100	
Foundations Of Mediaeval Europe	400	
Total		5000

	Sq. Ft.
Grand Total	35200

12. EUROPEAN CLUSTER

Introductory

The European Department's gallery proposals list over twenty individual galleries and period rooms for the display of British and Continental European decorative arts from the Middle Ages to the present day. The collection, which displays a wide range of techniques and stylistic change, contains examples of sculpture, architectural panelling, furniture, pottery and porcelain, glass, and metalwork. The individual components of the collection can be grouped logically in a series of divisions characterized by particular political, economic, and sociological forms, and also along chronological and cultural lines. It should be emphasized that the artistic history of Europe, as well as its development in other spheres did not take place in isolation, but was influenced by contacts with other parts of the world, most notably the Near and Far East and also, from the time of the 16th-century voyages of discovery, with parts of the New World.

While the gallery plans emphasize the development of style, the stylistic variations mirror the broader European culture in its totality through different stages of history.

Mediaeval Sculpture Gallery (Third Floor Rotunda)

Communication Objectives

To illustrate the stylistic changes from one period to another: barbaric styles being mainly ornamental; Romanesque being narrative in expression; Gothic, with architecture the dominant influence on fine and applied art, becoming enriched with humanistic expression in the 13th century.

To emphasize the fact that the Church was the only organized sponsor of the arts.

To show that Gothic, which took little hold in Italy, lingered in northern countries until the early 16th century, long after the Renaissance had appeared in Italy.

Religious sculptures show the change from the hieratic aloofness of Romanesque to the warmth and expression of the Gothic.

The English galleries, situated south of the Rotunda, will be arranged chronologically.

English Mediaeval Tudor to about 1600

Communication Objective

To illustrate the domestic and social setting of the English Mediaeval Tudor period.

A late 16th-century (Elizabethan) chamber, or withdrawing room, will show types and arrangements of the furniture, mainly oak, then in use. Accessory material in cases will give some idea of the quality of craftsmanship and of the methods of handling tools and materials. The influence of the Renaissance, which came late to England, will be discernible.

Early Stuart and Commonwealth, ca 1600-1660

Communication Objective

To demonstrate the historical development of furniture and pottery in early Stuart England.

The gallery will show prominent changes in furniture style, e.g., from the heavy panel-back chair to the more lightly constructed "Yorkshire-Derbyshire" type, and will examine regionalism in furniture styles and pottery.

Post-Restoration Stuart to about 1704

Communication Objective

To provide a dramatic demonstration of the revolution in taste in the English decorative arts after the restoration of Charles II, and its stimulation by fresh Continental influences, as well as by Oriental influences, via the East India Companies.

Silver shows the invigorating influence of first-generation Huguenot silversmiths on the existing English style. The glass collection exhibits the new English invention of lead glass, which stimulated an industry previously dependent mainly on imports.

Furniture will show the transition from oak to walnut and the introduction of new decorative techniques (veneering, caning, Japanning).

Queen Anne, ca 1704-1720

Communication Objectives

To show a cross-section of English decorative arts of the early years of the 18th century, primarily in the context of a small period room in the taste of relatively well-to-do city dweller or country gentleman.

To illustrate a now characteristic subdued and refined English classicism, influenced in part by French and more particularly by Dutch models, with an emphasis on plain, solid forms rather than on surface decoration.

To show the impact of England's growing maritime supremacy in terms of the influence of imports from the Far East and the adaptation of Far Eastern forms and motifs to items of native manufacture.

East-West Trade Gallery

Communication Objective

To demonstrate the importance of East-West trade, how the West perceived the Orient, and how those notions still affect us today.

The Asian export collections at the ROM are of international significance. Some of the themes which may be developed in this gallery include:

- trade fabrics from India (cotton chintz) and China (silks); also spices, tea;

- lacquer and porcelain and their European imitations;

- exotic luxuries of the Orient and their impact on the West:

- the Age of Discovery and how the West acquired knowledge about the Orient;

- effects of commerce on taste, technology, and human understanding;

- the notion of Cathay;

- comparison of Eastern wares and Western imitations (chinoiserie).

Early Georgian, ca 1720-1740

Communication Objective

To demonstrate a stylistic transition between Queen Anne and the Rococo period.

The introduction of mahogany, which in the mid-1720s began to overtake walnut in popularity, reinforced the taste for heavier and more elaborately decorated furniture. A pine-panelled room shows the new fashion of painting rooms in a pastel colour. Several large-scale carved tables show the relationship between monumental furniture style and English Palladian architecture, practised by architects such as William Kent.

Rococo, ca 1740-1770

Communication Objective

To show the extent to which the Rococo style influenced the decorative arts in England, and the three parts of the style: Gothic, Chinese, and Modern.

The furnishings of the "Weston Room", a mid-18th century pine-panelled library, illustrate the conscious assembling and collecting of *objects d'art*. Included will be objects demonstrating the emergence of English porcelain factories which derived their inspiration from Continental and Oriental prototypes. The influence of porcelain on earthenware and stoneware shows technical innovations that were part of the Industrial Revolution.

Late Georgian, ca 1770-1800

Communication Objective

To show Neoclassicism in England and internationally, and Neoclassic style as a reaction to the Rococo spirit.

This section will contain three period rooms: a drawing-room papered with English wallpaper in the Neoclassical style; a dining room of about 1800, also with papered walls, and showing furniture in a variety of designs of the period; and a bedroom area.

Regency and Victorian, ca 1800-1900

Communication Objective

To show Regency, an outgrowth of Neoclassical style, and its gradual dilution to the multitude of "styles" which make up Victorian style.

Regency furniture will be exhibited in several vignettes. A Victorian drawing-room with papered walls will show the overwhelming quantity and variety of material, much of it mass-produced, which was considered necessary to make life agreeable to the middle-class Victorian.

English Art Nouveau and 20th-Century

Communication Objectives

To show the applied arts in England from ca 1890 to the present.

To reveal certain uniquely English aspects of Art Nouveau.

This area will consist of six alcoves of furniture vignettes and accessory material.

Short-term Gallery

A shared space to be used for complementary displays.

The Continental galleries are located to the north of the Rotunda:

Lee Collection

Communication Objective

To illustrate a particular pattern or style of collecting which has its origins in the great religious and secular collections of the waning Middle Ages and in the Renaissance Kunst - or Schatzkammer.

Lent by the Massey Foundation, the Lee Collection must be displayed as a unit. As such, it communicates the story of one family's collection.

Renaissance, ca 1420-1540

Communication Objectives

To mark the beginning of the epoch which is considered "modern", a period in which harmony and balance are derived from classical qualities, and art is rendered with a fidelity to nature.

To show the distinction between northern and southern developments of this style.

Though furniture was still relatively sparse in the early Renaissance, it is hoped to create an interior or at least a vignette incorporating pieces of furniture and possibly carpet and fabrics with which interiors were embellished. Sculpture, metalwork, ceramics, and glass reinforce the new consciousness of the dignity of man and his works.

Mannerism, ca 1540-1620

Communication Objective

To focus on material which lies between Renaissance and Baroque, material which is noticeable for its elegant attenuation and frequent contortion, wilfully flouting the conventions established in the Renaissance.

An interior or vignette created around an Italian mantelpiece and containing furniture of the period will illustrate the theme. It will be amplified with ceramics (maiolica, including the important "Feast of the Wicked" plate), glass, sculpture, metalwork, and a large tapestry.

Baroque, ca 1620-1730

Communication Objectives

To display the material of the period in its context.

To show the boldness and elaborateness of furniture derived from architecture, and the imposing strength and unified movement of sculptures.

The material will be organized into French, German, and Central European Baroque, these being examples of the Baroque style as received from Italy.

Rococo, ca 1730-1770

Communication Objective

To show the strongest of all periods in French design and its influence on other Continental countries.

This gallery will contain a French Louis XV period room with panelled walls, together with other examples of furniture and decorative arts.

Louis XVI and Empire, ca 1770-1820

Communication Objectives

To emphasize the subtle differences between late Rococo and Neoclassicism in France, and the transformation of the latter style into the more archaeologically correct Empire style.

To show the Central European variations of these styles.

Biedermeier, Louis-Philippe, Second Empire, 1820-1885

Communication Objective

To show the difference between Central European and Western European furniture and applied arts.

French and German objects will be shown side-by-side to illustrate contrasting material tastes. German Biedermeier is the "clumsification" of Neoclassicism, and French Louis-Philippe is the imitation of mid-18th century French styles. The Second Empire, another French revival style, seeks inspiration in earlier periods.

Jugendstil and Continental 20th-Century

Communication Objective

To show distinctive national interpretations of Art Nouveau, and their source and interactions.

This area will include an early bedroom setting of the early 20th century and furniture and decorations showing the transition from Art Nouveau to Art Deco.

Costume Gallery

Communication Objectives

To exhibit the history of fashionable Western costume from 1650 to the present.

To present specific themes including regional or systematic exhibition related to costume history.

The content and organization of this gallery will change, but generally it will show the evolution of style in Western clothing as a reflection of social, cultural, economic, and technological developments.

European Arms and Armour Gallery

Communication Objective

To show an historical survey of European arms and armour from about 1200.

Linkages between this and the Costume gallery will be explored.

European Cluster

	Sq.Ft.	Sq.Ft.
Third Floor		
Introduction	200	
Short-term temporary	1200	
		1400
Mediaeval Sculpture Gallery	3100	
		3100
English Galleries (Total Less Textiles)	8500	
English Mediaeval Tudor		
Early Stuart and Commonwealth		
Post-Restoration Stuart		
Queen Anne		
East-West Trade	1000	
Early Georgian		
Rococo		
Late Georgian		
Regency and Victorian		
English Art Nouveau and 20th Century		
		9500
Continental Galleries (Total Less Subject)	5150	
Lee Collection	1000	
Renaissance		
Mannerism		
Baroque		
Rococo		
Louis XVI and Empire		
Biedermeier, Louis-Philippe, Second Empire		
Jugendstil and Continental 20th Century		
Costume Gallery	2400	
European Arms and Armour	2150	
		10700
Grand Total		24700

Part IV
Implementing the Plan

Part IV
Implementing the Plan

Successful galleries are the result of careful planning and
preparation. This section presents guidelines for implementing the plan in a way that should establish a climate of cre-
ativity and confidence.

This report is the second step in the creation of new galleries
at the ROM. In order to carry out the next phase effectively,
some operational policies are necessary, including a logical
process for the planning of galleries.

A. Guidelines for Developing Galleries:
A Visitor's Perspective

As a result of careful research over the last two years, many
interesting and helpful insights about the Museum visitor have
emerged. The following is a summary of the findings reviewed
earlier (Part II B). In order to provide a useful set of guidelines, the information has been divided into two parts, as answers to the following questions:

(1)   Who is the Museum visitor and how does he use the Museum?

(2)   What are the implications of the visitor profile for the
      development of galleries?

WHO IS THE MUSEUM VISITOR
AND HOW DOES HE USE THE EXISTING MUSEUM AND GALLERIES?

- The visitor to the ROM is intelligent and well-educated; he has a general interest in a wide range of subjects, and some intense particular interests.

- The visitor wants information, both simple and complex, but not necessarily technical.

- The visitor expects to learn, as well as to enjoy himself. He is prepared to learn in an unstructured context such as the Museum offers.

- The visitor is willing to spend considerable time on a Museum visit.

- The visitor usually comes to the Museum either in a peer group or in a family group.

- The visitor regards his visit as an occasion, one that is partly a learning experience, partly a social event.

- The visitor is usually a "museum-goer" with a general knowledge of what to expect in museums, but with little appreciation of the unique qualities of the ROM.

- The visitor visits the ROM in an orderly, but non-selective manner. He sees many galleries but reaches those on the third and lower levels less frequently than the others. He usually stops only at galleries that are of particular interest to him.

- The visitor is often confused and disoriented by lack of directions and by the layout of galleries.

- The visitor dislikes being crowded or uncomfortable (hot or tired); he appreciates a well-maintained gallery.

- The visitor likes artifacts and specimens and wants to be informed about the ones he sees; he frequently views the displays in a different way than do the curators.

- The visitor appreciates variety; he likes contrasts and drama, particularly presentations in the form of dioramas and habitats.

WHAT ARE THE IMPLICATIONS FOR THE DEVELOPMENT OF GALLERIES?

- All galleries can attract the Museum visitor, although some locations are likely to attract more people than others. Not all galleries are of interest to all visitors.

- Each gallery is competing for the visitor's attention and so must be designed in an appealing way.

- The part of a gallery encountered first often determines whether the visitor will explore further and how well he understands the subject matter.

- To assist his understanding, the visitor should be informed of the purpose and organization of a gallery.

- Information should be provided throughout the gallery to reinforce the initial message.

- Gallery design must ensure that the circulation path emphasizes the conceptual organization.

- A gallery area which is visually separate, clearly identified, and of manageable dimensions helps the visitor to understand its message.

- Routes through a gallery should be easy to follow, should avoid making the visitor backtrack, should enable him to decide whether to visit certain parts, and should provide attractions to maintain his interest. Entrances and exits should be positioned so as to prevent "short-circuiting".

- The circulation system needs to accommodate organized groups so that other visitors can comfortably bypass them. It must also ensure that popular exhibits can be viewed without creating "bottlenecks".

- Information to complement artifacts can be presented in different ways (labels, text panels, audio-visual techniques, graphics, and models). All should be used in a way that neither dominates nor conflicts with the objects.

- The information should be easily accessible and clearly linked to the exhibits.

- The type of information presented should take into account the fact that visitors may appreciate the academic significance of objects, but may also be interested in other aspects.

- Visitors should be informed of the unique qualities of collections or objects.

- The visitor should be made aware of research relevant to the artifacts or specimens on display.

- Where possible, presentations should build upon the visitor's knowledge and experience (e.g., moving from common insects to the more exotic).

- A clear indication that certain exhibits are temporary will help to evoke the image of a dynamic and changing Museum.

- Variety in the methods of display and in the objects selected helps to maintain visitor interest.

- Variations in presentation which are necessary to preserve artifacts (e.g., low lighting levels) should be explained to the visitor.

- Open displays can be effective but should include unambiguous indications of what can be touched and what cannot.

- Galleries should be clean and well maintained.

- When galleries or specific exhibits are known to be attractive to children (e.g., live displays), they should be designed with children's physical requirements in mind.

B. The Gallery Development Process

In early discussions with departments, it became apparent that
the methods and processes by which galleries are designed were
considered almost as important as the content. The approach
defined by the ECTF (outlined in *Opportunities and Constraints*) was
adopted as policy and has been guiding gallery development at
the ROM. Three galleries have already been planned using the
team concept defined in the report.

As a result of this experience, some modifications were made,
but the technique has proved generally successful and productive.
The description of the form of the team and the nature of the
process set out in *Opportunities and Constraints* are repeated below
in a slightly amended form.

GALLERY DEVELOPMENT TEAM

The development of a gallery is a complex undertaking, but it
is also potentially exciting and gratifying. Many people have
an interest in the outcome. The curator is concerned with presenting the subject matter accurately and adequately, the conservator with properly protecting the artifacts, the educator
with the effectiveness of the gallery as a learning experience,
and the designer with its aesthetics and impact. These are only
a few of the many considerations. To ensure that all essential
viewpoints are considered, a wide range of people must be involved in the process.

A Gallery Development Team (GDT) will be established to assume responsibility for shaping each new gallery. Every team will include core members, and will be chaired by the Head of the Exhibits Design Services Department. The core team should include representation from the following departments: curatorial, design, conservation, and education. To provide continuity, the same core people should, wherever possible, remain members of the team throughout the planning. At appropriate times the preparators, security and maintenance staff, and public relations staff should be involved.

The role of the team members will vary depending upon the nature of the particular problem in hand and the interests and capabilities of the individual. The team's purpose is to ensure that an appropriate mix of views is obtained, that views and concerns are presented at the appropriate times, and that a system of checks and balances is created which will reflect the disciplines and professions that constitute the team.

The interchange of opinions that occurs in a team situation is beneficial and useful in all contemplated gallery modifications. However, for minor changes that do not affect the original concept such consultation may be informal and limited. A pragmatic and responsible approach is required to prevent procedures from becoming an unreasonable burden, while at the same time ensuring that significant changes do not take place without proper consideration.

THE STAGES OF THE PROCESS

A sequence of decisions and activities is involved in the orderly development of a gallery or an exhibit. Some structuring is necessary to ensure that decisions are made at the appropriate times, that there is sufficient opportunity for reviewing objectives, and that budgets and schedules are met. The framework adopted consists of seven steps which should be followed in all important gallery changes:

(a)   initiation

(b)   communication objectives

(c)   the development of the overall design concept

(d)   programme

(e)   design

(f)   implementation

(g)   evaluation and follow-up.

(a)   INITIATION

The first step in the creation of a gallery is the submission of a proposal. Usually, this will be made by a curatorial depart-ment, although it could be made by a group of departments or even the Exhibits and Gallery Communications Committee (EGCC). A proposal should include a preliminary statement of purpose and of the message to be conveyed: it should also give an estimate of the amount of space required.

This step was included when the overall gallery plan for the ROM was developed. Proposals were obtained from all depart-ments and allocations of space were made. Section E of this Part (Priorities, Schedules, and Budgets), includes schedules and budgets for the first major stage of gallery development. For every gallery project a Gallery Development Team will be es-tablished. Each team will be given a precise allocation of space, a preliminary budget, and a schedule for completion.

(b)   COMMUNICATION OBJECTIVES

The second stage is the elaboration of the concepts for each gallery; these are best expressed in a series of specific communication objectives. The main responsibility for trans-lating the preliminary statement of purpose into a set of communication objectives lies with the curatorial members of the team, but they must work closely with other members of the core team, since the objectives establish the basic direction for a gallery.

If communication objectives are clearly defined, the content of an exhibit can be designed so as to get its message across clear-ly to the visitor. He must be made explicitly aware of what the exhibit is about, how it is organized, what he can learn from it and—perhaps most important of all—what it has to do with him. Students are guided towards the answers to these questions by teachers; the casual visitor is often left to guess at them.

An explicit statement of objectives will not only ensure that all members of a Gallery Development Team have the same understanding of a job to be done, but will also provide an important guide for decision-making throughout the remainder of the process.

(c)   THE DEVELOPMENT OF THE OVERALL DESIGN CONCEPT

In this phase, the curator(s), designer, conservator, educator, and, if necessary, an editor work together to develop a concept that will reflect the communication objectives. This concept must be based upon a firm understanding of the strengths and limitations of the collection, the amount and kind of space available, the budget, and the schedule. The development of the concept requires an understanding of the physical form the gallery will take, the major elements and their arrangement, the focal point of the gallery, and the display methods to be used (free-standing cases, wall-mounted cases, live exhibits, audio-visuals, etc.).

(d)   PROGRAMME

The overall design concept is expanded into a programme which includes a script of what is to be said, a list of artifacts or specimens, and support material. At this point, a more precise budget and schedule can be established.

(e)   DESIGN

Now the main burden shifts to the designers as the team prepares a detailed design for the gallery. This can be most effectively demonstrated by a large-scale working model. In some instances more elaborate finished gallery models may be useful for other purposes (obtaining grants, publicity, education). Countless design decisions must be made during this stage, all of which must be compatible with the artifacts and specimens and with the intent of the programme. Consultation with preparators and maintenance and security staff is particularly useful at this stage. Final budgets and schedules must be drawn up at this point.

(f)   IMPLEMENTATION

At this stage, the work is carried out primarily by the Exhibit Design Services Department. The GDT must work with the head of this department to resolve problems and to ensure that no changes or adjustments are made without approval.

(g)   EVALUATION AND FOLLOW-UP

Evaluation is more than simply a stage of the work; it is an integral part of the whole process of gallery development. It should be continuous, providing a point of reference for all decisions, rather than just an independent comment on the results. The formative evaluation depends upon the initial definition of communication objectives.

Evaluation also involves testing. Certain ideas or techniques may require pre-testing even before a gallery opens. After the gallery is completed, the evaluation must be able to identify problems and to initiate necessary improvements. Without this corrective function, evaluation would result merely in frustration.

A further purpose of evaluation is to build a body of knowledge and experience from which future galleries can benefit. All evaluation activities should be carefully documented and made available to those involved in subsequent gallery projects.

The setting of objectives and the testing of their accomplishments will reveal the strengths and weaknesses of galleries and of gallery proposals. The identification of weaknesses should be viewed as a learning experience, not as evidence of failure. Attempts to communicate a new idea or to use a novel technique always involve risks. Some experiments will produce exciting results, others will not. Evaluation should enable such ventures to be undertaken with a higher assurance of success. When gallery projects are successful, members of the team should receive public recognition.

Supplementary Information

In addition to creating and evaluating a gallery, the GDT should consider the nature and form of supplementary information. Brochures, orientation information, and gallery guides should express the communication objectives.

Curatorial Responsibility

The development of a gallery requires substantial time commitments. It can be particularly demanding for representatives of curatorial departments whose time and energy are distributed over a wide range of responsibilities. Departmental resources, already strained, will inevitably be affected. However, without a serious commitment from curatorial representatives, galleries cannot be created. Before the work proceeds, the department(s) will have to recognize that much curatorial time will be required, and the administration that other undertakings by the department during the period will be curtailed.

Curatorial departments are not expected to supply all the technical assistance required to create a gallery. If technical contributions on a large scale are needed (e.g., taxidermy in a major mammalogy gallery), they will be provided for in the gallery budget. Moreover, where other departments are obliged to provide extensive special assistance (e.g., the Conservation Department will require one and a half man-years of work to consolidate mummy cases before standing them upright), this also will be budgeted as part of the cost. Such budgeting procedures will only be adopted when the tasks would seriously interfere with the regular work of a department.

ADDENDUM TO PART IVB

November 1978

Since the writing of this report some six months ago, the
ROM has completed several projects using the seven-stage
process. As a result of this experience, the process has
been reviewed and modified. It is now felt that greater
efficiency in the development of a gallery can be achieved
by telescoping some of the stages. This will create a more
organic process rather than a sequential one.

The stages of the process are now structured as follows:

(a)   Programme

(b)   Negotiation

(c)   Detailed Package

(d)   Approval

(e)   Implementation

(f)   Evaluation

(a)   PROGRAMME STAGE

The programme stage is equivalent to a first draft of a manu-
script. During this stage the Gallery Development Team under-
takes the development of the communication objectives, overall
design concept, and programme for a gallery. The product at
the end of this stage includes overall and individual communication objectives, rough draft of the gallery text, lists of
specimens or artifacts, drawings, a scale model, and a first
estimate of costs. This allows the GDT to deal with all
aspects of a gallery before submitting any one part for review
and approval.

(b)   NEGOTIATION STAGE

The negotiation stage will involve discussion between the
Gallery Development Team and the Exhibit and Gallery Communications Committee (EGCC), when the gallery programme is
reviewed. At this point either the programme is returned
to the committee for further clarification or approval is
given for the GDT to proceed to the next stage.

(c)   DETAILED PACKAGE STAGE

Upon approval of the programme by the EGCC, the GDT will undertake the final planning. This will include specific copy,
graphics, final lists of specimens or artifacts, working
drawings, and a detailed costing. In addition, a detailed
model may be necessary at this time.

(d)   APPROVAL STAGE

Once the GDT has completed work on the detailed package, the
team meets again with the EGCC to review all the components.
When approval is given, the project is scheduled and the GDT
then has its mandate to proceed with the implementation.

(e)   IMPLEMENTATION STAGE

The implementation stage consists of the physical development
and construction of the gallery. The process as outlined
earlier is applicable here.

(f)   EVALUATION STAGE

The evaluation stage has not been modified and is fully described
in the earlier description of the process.

C. The Role of the Exhibit and Gallery Communications Committee (EGCC)

The gallery development programme defined in the Section E (Priorities, Schedules, and Budgets) requires careful monitoring and coordination. As the first series of galleries will be developed simultaneously, it will be necessary to ensure that the planned relationships between them are maintained, that human resources are allocated reasonably, and that budgets and schedules are met.

The ECTF recommended in its *Opportunities and Constraints* Report that:

> A standing committee of the Museum (Exhibit and Gallery Communications Committee) be established on a permanent basis to implement the Overall Plan for Galleries. This committee should consist of staff drawn from a wide spectrum of museum expertise and interest. The responsibilities of the committee should include the monitoring and evaluation of all exhibit activity and the review of the policies of the Museum in the light of the effectiveness of these activities.

This recommendation was approved by the Director. The Exhibit and Gallery Communication Committee (EGCC) will be established with the tabling of this report.

The EGCC will monitor the work of all Gallery Development Teams throughout the programme, using the review procedures already described. EGCC approval will be required at the completion of each of the following stages: Stage 2, Communication Objectives; Stage 3, Overall Design Concept; Stage 4, Programme; Stage 5, Design. When a gallery is completed and evaluated, a thorough report on the successes and failures of the project (especially with reference to any modifications) is to be submitted to the EGCC.

A further role of the EGCC will be to oversee the work of the Temporary Exhibits Committee (TEC). The TEC will prepare an annual schedule of all temporary exhibits for review and approval by the EGCC. This will ensure that a reasonable balance is maintained in the allocation of human and financial resources between new gallery development and temporary exhibits.

The Temporary Exhibits Committee will be responsible for the scheduling of all exhibits within Exhibition Hall and the adjacent atrium area, and for coordinating displays in the temporary galleries within clusters. Although these temporary galleries are primarily for the use of departments within clusters, up to 30% of their use may be devoted to external shows under the auspices of the Temporary Exhibits Committee. Such shows would be subject to approval by the departments within the relevant cluster.

Temporary displays within departmental galleries can impose a strain on available resources. To facilitate the allocation of resources, all temporary displays within departmental or multidisciplinary galleries which require non-curatorial assistance are to be coordinated through the TEC.

The TEC will be requested to submit its first schedule by September 15, 1978, to cover the period to June 30, 1979. Thereafter, each January from January of 1979, the TEC will submit an annual schedule covering the coming year from July 1 to June 30.

Apart from this annual review of its overall level of activity and the identification of major tasks throughout the year, the TEC will function independently. However, any significant changes in schedules or new projects considered by the TEC must be submitted to the EGCC.

D. Signage

The importance of signage as part of the orientation system has been discussed earlier. One further aspect must be mentioned here.

Early in its deliberations the ECTF adopted a policy of providing French as well as English signs for public information such as the location of facilities and any safety notices. This policy has been approved by the Director. However, because it was felt that bilingual gallery signage would become too complex, it will not be used.

E. Priorities, Schedules, and Budgets

The ROM plan for its galleries is a major undertaking. New gallery space is being added and all existing galleries will be disrupted by the renovations necessary to improve the environmental conditions and to replace the entire mechanical and electrical systems in the present building.

This part of the report presents a proposed schedule for the next eighteen years. The first phase is integrated with the renovation and expansion programme, and is directed towards completing the first set of galleries in time for the re-opening of the Museum. The second phase is a series of minor renovations, and the third phase completes the new gallery development programme. This programme is based upon the staff and financial resources expected to be available during the developmental period.

Phase I includes the development of seven main gallery areas (comprising approximately 55,000 square feet), and Exhibition Hall (an additional 9,000 square feet), to be ready when the Museum re-opens in 1982.

Priority has been given to those areas which are to be located in the Terrace galleries. This space will become available for installation approximately thirteen months before the renovation project is completed.

Phase II consists of minor renovations to existing displays and will allow the Museum to re-open 45,000 square feet of gallery space fairly quickly. Included in Phase II will be the existing Vertebrate Fossils and Invertebrate Fossils galleries on Level 2 (East Wing), and the Mammalogy, Ornithology, Arthropod, and Ichthyology and Herpetology galleries on Level 3 (East Wing). These galleries will be largely restored to their present status after the renovations to these areas. The fourth gallery will be located on Level 2 of the Terrace galleries and will contain displays from the Egyptian, Greek and Roman, and West Asian galleries. It will be a relocation of existing cases and displays (e.g., the mummies) which are at present on exhibit on Level 2. These galleries will be organized into a new temporary display.

With the completion of Phases I and II, a total of 108,000 square feet of gallery space will be available to the public.

Phase III envisages the completion of the gallery development programme with the provision of another 150,000 square feet of permanent gallery space, and will include the upgrading of the 43,000 square feet temporarily refurbished in Phase II. This phase will take a number of years and will be undertaken as financial resources become available.

The galleries in Phase III are listed in the order in which they will be developed. This order is based on the following system of priorities:

First priority   -   galleries not included in Phases I or II, e.g., Earth Sciences.

Second priority   -   galleries proposed for the Centre Block and Terrace galleries, e.g., Invertebrate galleries.

Third priority   -   galleries that must be relocated before other galleries can be undertaken, e.g., Mammalogy and Ornithology.

Fourth priority   -   galleries located in the north-west wing, as this space is to be used for interim storage of collections, e.g., Far East and Botany.

Fifth priority   -   galleries with major existing displays e.g., Vertebrate Fossils.

The budget for the various galleries is calculated on a square-footage basis ranging from $25.00 to $100.00, depending upon the type of gallery. All the calculations are based on 1978 dollars.

Table IV: Summary of Schedule Development

MONTHS

Phase I

Discovery Galleries (Level B2-Terrace)	32
New World (Level B1-Terrace)	38
Europe/Canada (Level B1-Terrace)	38
Mankind Discovering (Level 1-Centre Block)	41
Far East (Level 1-Terrace)	38
Life Science Interdisciplinary (Level 2-Centre Block)	41
Ancient World (Level 3-Terrace)	38
Exhibition Hall (Level 1-SE Wing)	28

Phase II

Vertebrate Fossils (Level 2-NE Wing)	2
Invertebrate Fossils (Level 2-SE Wing)	2
Life Sciences (Level 3-East Wing)	2
Ancient World (Level 2-Terrace)	6

Phase III

Earth Sciences (Level 1-SW Wing)	44
Life Science Interdisciplinary (Level 2-Centre Block)	36
Mammalogy (Level 2-SW Wing)	48
Europe/Canada (Level 3-NE Wing)	44
Ancient World (Level 3-West Wing)	48
Invertebrate Galleries (Level 2-Terrace)	46
New World (Level B1-Centre Block)	38
Old World Ethnology (Level B1-Centre Block)	36
Herpetology (Level 2-SE Wing)	36
Ornithology (Level 2-SE Wing)	36
Botany (Level 2-NW Wing)	32
Ichthyology (Level 2-NW Wing)	36
Mammalogy (Level 2-NW Wing)	36
Far East (Level 1-NW Wing)	34
Europe/Canada (Level 3-SE Wing)	44
Planetarium (Planetarium)	40
Vertebrate Fossils (Level 2-NE Wing)	30

Table VI: Budget Summary of Gallery Development Phases

	Sq. Ft.	Cost*
Phase I		
Discovery Galleries (Level B2-Terrace)	2,780	$ 69,500
New World (Level B1-Terrace)	8,925	468,300
Europe/Canada (Level B1-Terrace)	7,350	514,500
Mankind Discovering (Level 1-Centre Block)	7,500	675,000
Far East (Level 1-Terrace)	17,600	894,000
Life Science Disciplinary (Level 2-Centre Block)	3,500	315,000
Ancient World (Level 3-Terrace)	6,700	469,000
Exhibition Hall**	9,250	$ 185,000
Atrium space adjacent to Exhibition Hall	4,550	
Phase I Sub-total	68,155	$ 3,590,300
Phase II		
Vertebrate Fossils (Level 2-NE Wing)		$ 15,000
Invertebrate Fossils (Level 2-SE Wing)		5,000
Life Sciences (Level 3-East Wing)		30,000
Ancient World (Level 2-Terrace)		75,000
Phase II Sub-total		$ 125,000
Phase III		
Earth Sciences (Level 1-SW Wing)	15,600	$ 1,560,000
Life Science Interdisciplinary (Level 2-Centre Block)	4,000	360,000
Mammalogy (Level 2-SW Wing)	10,000	1,000,000
Europe/Canada (Level 3-NE Wing)	15,800	1,185,000
Ancient World (Level 3-West Wing)	28,500	2,137,500
Invertebrate Galleries (Level 2-Terrace)	10,440	1,044,000
New World (Level B1-Centre Block)	6,075	364,500
Old World Ethnology (Level B1-Centre Block)	2,750	165,000

---

*All costs are in 1978 dollars.

**These costs are for the preparation of Exhibition Hall and do not include costs for the opening exhibition.

	Sq. Ft.	Cost
Herpetology (Level 2-SE Wing)	3,360	336,000
Ornithology (Level SE Wing)	3,360	336,000
Botany (Level 2-NW Wing)	2,520	252,000
Ichthyology (Level 2-NW Wing)	2,750	275,000
Mammalogy (Level 2-NW Wing)	5,000	500,000
Far East (Level 1-NW Wing)	12,380	742,800
Europe/Canada (Level 3-SE Wing)	10,850	813,750
Planetarium (Planetarium)	7,500	600,000
Vertebrate Fossils (Level 2-NE Wing)	10,720	350,000
Phase III Sub-total		
	151,605	$12,021,550
Overall Totals	219,760	$15,736,850

Appendices

Appendix A: Floor Plans of the Existing Building

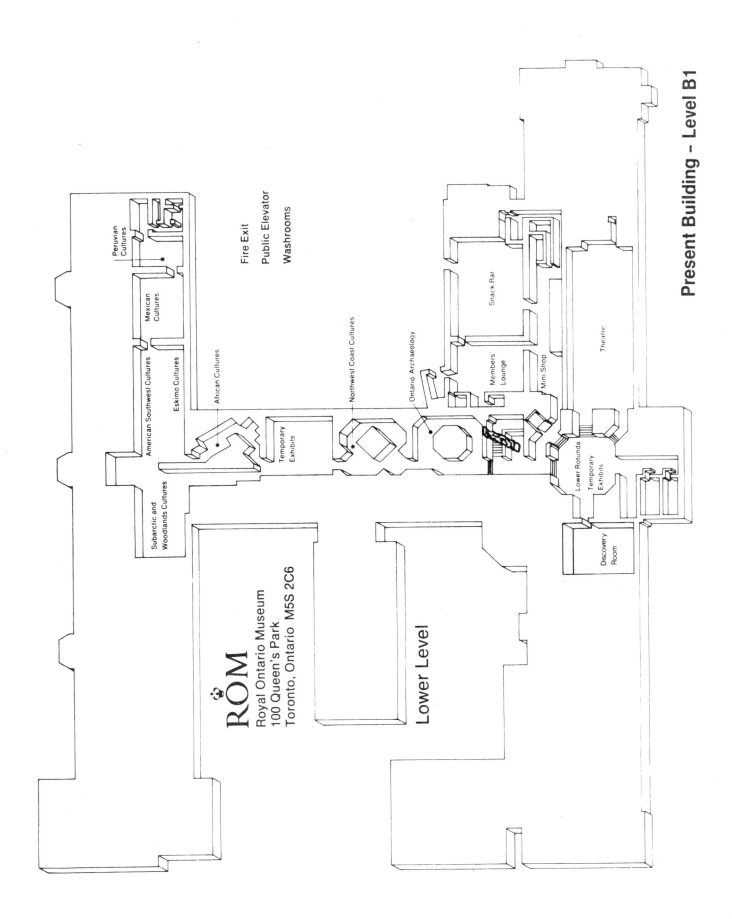

Present Building - Level B1

ROM
Royal Ontario Museum
100 Queen's Park
Toronto, Ontario M5S 2C6

Lower Level

Fire Exit
Public Elevator
Washrooms

Peruvian Cultures
Mexican Cultures
American Southwest Cultures
Eskimo Cultures
Subarctic and Woodlands Cultures
African Cultures
Temporary Exhibits
Northwest Coast Cultures
Ontario Archaeology
Members' Lounge
Snack Bar
Mini Shop
Lower Rotunda
Temporary Exhibits
Discovery Room
Theatre

194

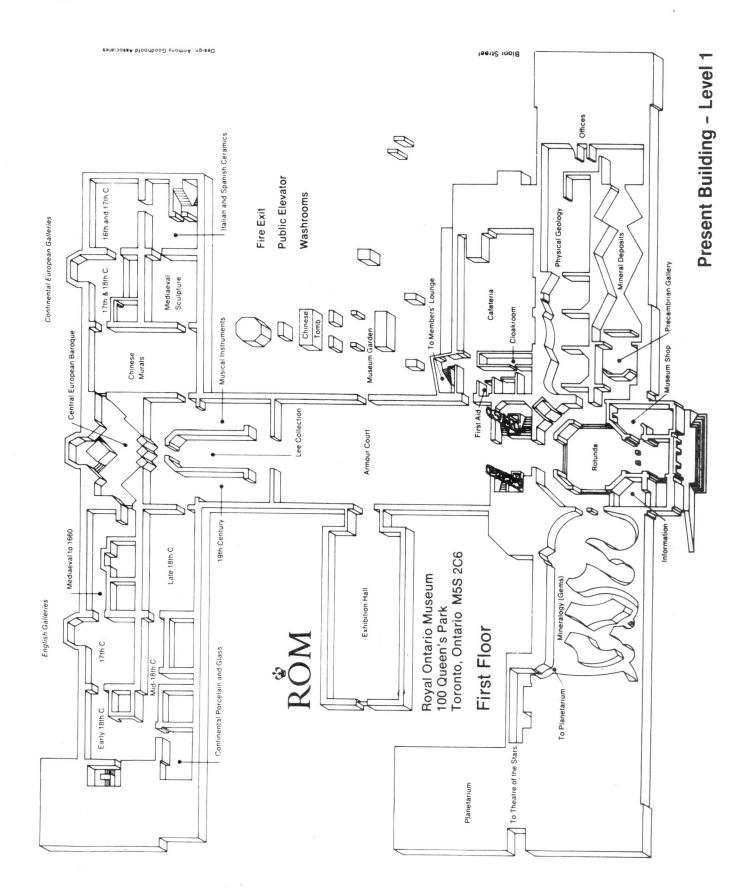

Present Building – Level 1

Bloor Street

Offices

Physical Geology

Mineral Deposits

Cafeteria

Cloakroom

Museum Shop

Precambrian Gallery

First Aid

To Members' Lounge

Rotunda

Information

Mineralogy (Gems)

To Planetarium

Planetarium

To Theatre of the Stars

Design Anthony Goodhoold Associates

Continental European Galleries

16th and 17th C.

17th & 18th C.

Mediaeval Sculpture

Chinese Murals

Central European Baroque

Italian and Spanish Ceramics

Fire Exit

Public Elevator

Washrooms

Chinese Tomb

Museum Garden

Musical Instruments

Lee Collection

Armour Court

English Galleries

Mediaeval to 1660

17th C.

Mid-18th C.

Late 18th C.

19th Century

Early 18th C.

Continental Porcelain and Glass

ROM

Exhibition Hall

Royal Ontario Museum
100 Queen's Park
Toronto, Ontario M5S 2C6

First Floor

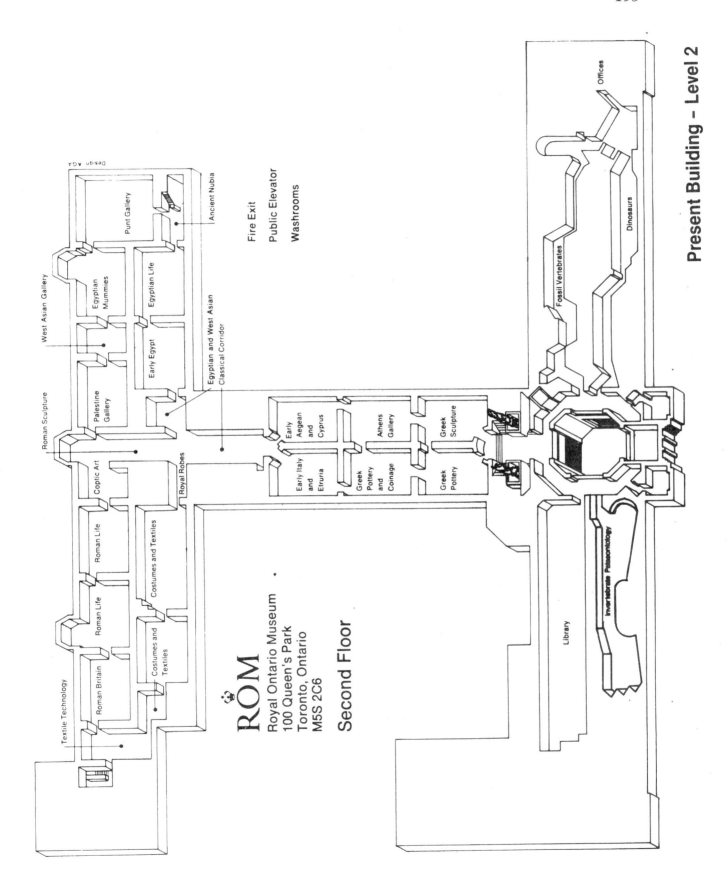

Present Building – Level 2

ROM

Royal Ontario Museum
100 Queen's Park
Toronto, Ontario
M5S 2C6

Second Floor

Fire Exit

Public Elevator

Washrooms

Textile Technology
Roman Britain
Roman Life
Roman Life
Coptic Art
Roman Sculpture
Costumes and Textiles
Costumes and Textiles
Royal Robes
Palestine Gallery
West Asian Gallery
Early Egypt
Egyptian Life
Egyptian Mummies
Punt Gallery
Design AGA
Ancient Nubia
Egyptian and West Asian
Classical Corridor
Early Aegean and Cyprus
Early Italy and Etruria
Athens Gallery
Greek Pottery and Coinage
Greek Sculpture
Greek Pottery
Library
Invertebrate Palaeontology
Fossil Vertebrates
Dinosaurs
Offices

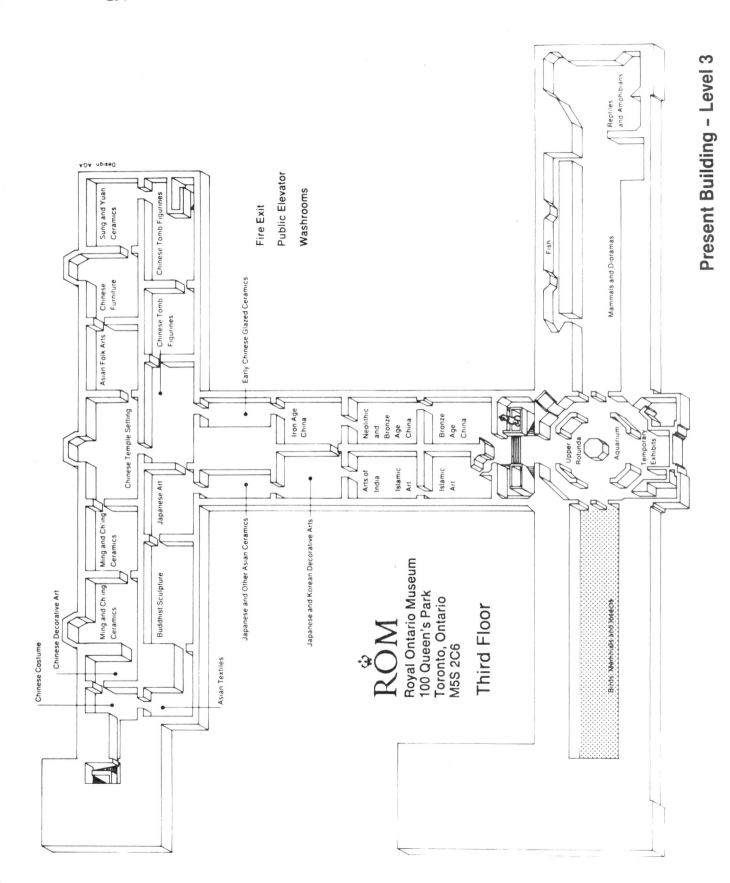

Present Building – Level 3

Chinese Costume
Chinese Decorative Art
Ming and Ch'ing Ceramics
Ming and Ch'ing Ceramics
Buddhist Sculpture
Asian Textiles

Sung and Yuan Ceramics
Chinese Furniture
Asian Folk Arts
Chinese Temple Setting
Japanese Art

Chinese Tomb Figurines
Chinese Tomb Figurines
Design AGA

Early Chinese Glazed Ceramics
Japanese and Other Asian Ceramics
Japanese and Korean Decorative Arts

Iron Age China
Neolithic and Bronze Age China
Arts of India
Islamic Art
Bronze Age China
Islamic Art

Upper Rotunda
Aquarium
Temporary Exhibits

Fish
Mammals and Dioramas
Reptiles and Amphibians
Birds, Mammals and Insects

Fire Exit
Public Elevator
Washrooms

RŌM
Royal Ontario Museum
100 Queen's Park
Toronto, Ontario
M5S 2C6

Third Floor

Appendix B: Selected ECTF Bulletins

♔ ROM   E.C.T.F. BULLETIN   NO. 1

EXHIBITS COMMUNICATIONS TASK FORCE

J. Di Profio; Chairman

L. Levine; Vice Chairman   Date: October 15, 1976

This is the first of a series of Bulletins which will be issued by the ECTF. We do not mean to further burden you with material to read, but this is our only way of keeping you informed about progress of the ECTF, and of ensuring your constant feedback.

The purpose of this first Bulletin is to describe to you our work program. As the Director indicated in his memorandum about the ECTF (No. 42), we are charged with drawing up a master plan for communicating with the museum visitor. It will take approximately 18 months to complete this plan, and the accompanying diagram is a graphic presentation of activities and deadlines which the ECTF has set itself.

As part of the work, we will approach all departments in the Museum for their ideas and help. Two formal review periods have been scheduled, but suggestions and queries are, of course, welcome at any time. All comments that might be relevant to the theme of communication, be it through galleries, public spaces, temporary exhibits, lectures, tours, or indeed any area of concern within this broad spectrum, should be directed to the chairman, or to one of the committee members.

The accompanying diagram indicates some key dates. These deadlines are imposed on us by the building program, and we will have to adhere to these rather strictly. We would like to draw some of these dates to your attention.

o The investigative activities of the ECTF must be completed by April 1, 1977.

o We will produce a report of the investigative activities by June 1, 1977 for consideration by all staff, and would like responses to this report by July 1, 1977.

o A second review period is scheduled during January 1978 to consider a preliminary draft of the Communications Master Plan.

Jan Schroer of the ECTF office (Ext. 5429) is always available to explain our work and to receive any comments from you.

Logic Diagram of ECTF Activities (With ECTF Bulletin #1)

200

Timeline headers: OCT. 1 | 76   APRIL 1 | 77   JUNE 1 | 77 : JULY 1 | 77   OCT. 1 | 77   JAN. 1 | 78 : FEB. 1 | 78

ONGOING / PLANNING / DESIGN

WORK OF PROJECT OFFICE

WORK OF THEME WORK GROUP

WORK OF DISCOVERY ROOM WORK GROUP

WORK OF THE EXHIBITS COMMUNICATIONS TASK FORCE

PRELIMINARY INVESTIGATIVE ACTIVITIES:
- DEVELOP ATTENDANCE DATA
- ON-GOING LITERATURE REVIEW
- DEVELOP VISITOR PROFILE INFORMATION
- UNDERTAKE GALLERY EVALUATION
- ASSESS PHYSICAL PLANNING IMPLICATIONS
- IDENTIFY OPERATIONAL ISSUES

ASSESSMENT & REPORT OF OPPORTUNITIES & CONSTRAINTS

DEVELOPMENT OF BASIC CONSIDERATIONS FOR COMMUNICATIONS MASTER PLAN
- PURPOSE & OBJECTIVES
- CONCEPTUAL CONSIDERATIONS
- PHYSICAL CONSIDERATIONS
- OPERATIONAL CONSIDERATIONS

PRELIMINARY DRAFT EXHIBITS COMMUNICATIONS MASTER PLAN

EXPERIMENTAL PROJECTS

REVIEW BY ALL

FINAL DRAFT C.M.P.

INTRODUCTION
PURPOSE & OBJECTIVES

1) MUSEUM-WIDE CONCEPTUAL CONSIDERATIONS
- IMAGE / ARRIVAL
- USE OF THEME
OVERALL APPROACH TO:
- ORIENTATION
- EDUCATION
- GALLERIES / PUBLIC AREAS

2) INDIVIDUAL GALLERY CONCEPTUAL CONSIDERATIONS
- USE OF THEME
- APPROACH TO:
  - ORIENTATION
  - EDUCATION
  - DIDACTIC INFO
  - DISCOVERY TOOL

3) PHYSICAL CONSIDERATIONS
- QUALITIES OF BLDG.
- EXPANSION / PHASING
- SPATIAL ALLOCATION OF GALLERIES / PUBLIC AREAS
- GENERAL PRIORITIES
- CIRCULATION MUSEUM / INDIVIDUAL GALLERIES

4) OPERATIONAL CONSIDERATIONS
- STAFF / VISITOR RELATIONSHIP
- MAINTENANCE
- SECURITY
- CONSERVATION

SPECIFIED TASKS & OTHER CONTRIBUTIONS

REVIEW BY ALL

SPECIFIED TASKS & OTHER CONTRIBUTIONS

CONTRIBUTING DEPARTMENTS:
- CURATORIAL
- EDUCATION
- EXTENSION
- TECHNOLOGY
- PUBLIC RELATIONS
- DESIGN SERVICES
- CONSERVATION
- PREPARATORS
- MAINTENANCE
- SECURITY
- EXHIBITS COMMITTEE

E.C.T.F. BULLETIN

201 ROM

EXHIBITS COMMUNICATIONS TASK FORCE   NO. 4

J. Di Profio; Chairman
L. Levine; Vice Chairman   Date: March 30, 1977

For the past five months the Exhibits Communications Task
Force has been pursuing the work programme adopted last
October and outlined to you in our first bulletin. The
purpose of this bulletin is to report on our progress and
in particular to draw to your attention activities which
will create some physical changes in the building in the
near future.

Before outlining our work, we would like to clarify several
points. There seems to be some confusion between the role
of the ECTF (Renovation and Expansion Planning Group 2) and
the role of the architects and their consultants (Renovation
and Expansion Planning Group 1). The ECTF operates independently of the architectural planning group. The ECTF is concerned with planning for galleries; the architectural group
is concerned with the planning of all new building facilities
and mechanical renovation to all present spaces. The work of
the two groups is necessarily co-ordinated through the Project
Office. Although the ECTF is an internal task force, we have
retained outside consulting staff to assist us in our work.
Many of you have met Mr. Henry Sears, who is the staff coordinator for the ECTF, and Betty Kaser who assists him.
For a detailed description of the ECTF and its terms of
reference, please refer to Director's Memorandum #42.

Gallery Renovations

An "Interim Guidelines for Gallery Renovations" was adopted
by the ECTF in November, 1976 as the basis for considering
renovation proposals prior to the completion of a detailed
plan for Exhibit Communications. A number of proposals,
based on these guidelines, have been recommended to the
Director for approval. Renovations to the Egyptian and
European galleries have been approved fully. In addition,
approval in principle has been given to renovations to the
Ichthyology and Herpetology gallery and to the Arthropod
gallery.

Planning is underway for other areas. Communications Design
Teams have been established to develop concepts for an
Invertebrate Palaeontology Gallery (D. Collins - Chairman),
and an Introductory Natural Sciences Gallery (R. Peterson -
Chairman). In addition, some housekeeping is under way on
the 3rd floor.

ECTF Work Groups

Four Work Groups were established by the ECTF to undertake
specific tasks. The Student Entry Work Group (R. Moynes -
Chairman) was formed to recommend plans for improving the
reception of school groups entering the Museum. The work
of this group has been completed and a plan to permit student
entrance via the postern stairwell is now being implemented.
The following changes will take place: provision of a paved
staging area immediately to the south of the main entrance
to the building; improvements to the postern stairwell; the
provision of new student coat facilities on the lower floor
opposite the postern stairwell (in the area now used as storage
for the shops). These changes also involve some adjustments
to the Museum theatre. It will be shortened by moving the
stage forward about 20', reducing seating capacity from about
450 to 350, but improving the general appearance somewhat.
The space made available by this adjustment will enable shop
storage and maintenance facilities to be provided in that area.
These improvements are scheduled for completion by June, 1977.
The theatre itself will be closed for renovations from April 4
until May 15.

The Museum Visitor Reception Work Group (J. Lavery - Chairman)
was established to investigate and recommend improvements to
the entrance Rotunda and other public areas of the Museum.
The Work Group has presented an interim report which has been
given preliminary approval by the Director. Basically their
recommendations focus upon the centralization of all reception
functions (cashier, information, reception and membership) into
a core desk system situated in the centre of the Rotunda; and
secondly, upon the development of a signage and orientation
system. Stage 1 of their recommendations, which has received
final approval from the Director, involves immediate improvements to the public washrooms, relocation of the Ontario Scene
Board, development of a signage system, and the provision of
improved storage for baby strollers, umbrellas and other such
items.

The Discovery Room Work Group (R. Moynes - Chairman) has
recommended that an experimental discovery room be developed
to evaluate the discovery room concept. The recommendation
has been approved by the Director and Room 4 on the lower
level will be used for this purpose. The experimental room
is scheduled to be opened around the beginning of July. Room
4 will be unavailable for other uses from May 15, 1977.

The Theme Work Group (T. C. Young - Chairman) was charged
with the responsibility of investigating the theme concept and
possible applications of a theme for the Museum. Their
deliberations are still in progress, and a report will be
submitted to the ECTF on April 1, 1977.

Investigative Activities

The ECTF has undertaken a series of investigations related to
the future planning of galleries. Interviews with all curatorial and many non-curatorial departments, to solicit views
and concerns about galleries, have been completed. In addition,
surveys are underway to draw up a profile of the ROM visitor
and investigate the patterns of use of the Museum by visitors.
The results of these surveys will be presented in our first
report to the Museum. As indicated in our first bulletin,
this report is scheduled for distribution to Museum staff
at the beginning of June.

E.C.T.F. BULLETIN

EXHIBITS COMMUNICATIONS TASK FORCE

J. Di Profio; Chairman

L. Levine; Vice Chairman

NO. 5

Date: November 20, 197

The past few months have been a time of very intensive work for the ECTF. All gallery proposals from the curatorial departments have now been received and reviewed by members of the ECTF. As many of you are aware, in some instances additional interviews have been held with departments to obtain further information or clarification of specific aspects of their proposals. In other instances, the information presented was sufficient so as not to require an interview at this time. First then, we would like to thank all curatorial departments for the considerable effort put forth at this very busy time to complete gallery proposal forms. Both individually and collectively, the ideas presented promise exciting possibilities for better communication with the Museum's public.

As a result of our review of the gallery proposals, we have now developed some working principles by which we can continue with our task. Once again, we will need the assistance and cooperation of curatorial departments in moving to the next stage. In order to provide some common ground for the work which we will collectively have to perform over the next few months, we are using this bulletin to inform you of our current thinking. The information presented is in two parts - the first relates to departmental galleries and the second to interdisciplinary and general galleries.

DEPARTMENTAL GALLERIES

We have taken the information from the gallery proposals that suggests desired relationships between galleries (both within and beyond departments) and developed charts of these gallery interrelationships. Two charts are appended to this bulletin - one for the science departments and one for the art and archaeology departments.

The circles in the charts represent departmental gallery concepts as proposed. The lines connecting various galleries and departments represent the relationships between galleries that individual departments have indicated were most important. The charts are intended to illustrate these relationships in an orderly form, and to indicate logical clusters of galleries which flow from these relationships.

Several points should be kept in mind when looking at these charts:

(1) These are preliminary working diagrams, intended to provide a basis for discussion with departments. To date, individual departments have not had the opportunity to consider their gallery proposals in relationship to all other departmental proposals. There is nothing sacred about any of the information presented. As a result of examining the overall picture, you may wish to alter your proposal, make suggestions regarding different relationships, or to comment on the interpretations derived from the proposals submitted. The purpose of these charts is to stimulate such response.

(2) The way in which departments have been clustered is also provisional. Preliminary discussion with respect to clusters has already taken place with some departments and changes have been proposed. The titles given to clusters of departments are similarly working titles.

(3) The size of boxes and the number of circles bear no relationship to space. The charts are conceptual and concerned with relationships, not space. No space allocations have been made.

(4)   The charts do not include suggestions for inter-
       disciplinary galleries other than those which have
       been proposed as part of the gallery proposals of
       some departments.

There is value in developing a physical arrangement of galleries
in a way which makes sense for individual departments and
also provides a more logical orientation for the visitor. The
ECTF has decided to use the concept of forming clusters of
closely related galleries (the charts present a preliminary
suggestion) as the basis for arranging galleries. Your comments
on this initial attempt at clusters are welcomed.

You will note that some gallery requests currently fall outside
the clusters. For example, the Textiles Department has requested
gallery space that would relate their collections to several
clusters. The Ethnology Department has some collections which
do not fall precisely into any of the clusters identified, e.g.,
Africa. These situations will be dealt with in the development
of an overall gallery plan which is the next phase of our work.

INTERDISCIPLINARY AND GENERAL GALLERIES

In addition to looking at the arrangement of departmental
galleries, the ECTF has been examining interdisciplinary
galleries from the point of view of the ideas proposed
and the relationship of these ideas to departmental galleries.
As a result of this examination, two aspects of such galleries
have been discussed in some detail - location and duration.
With respect to location, it is evident that some of these
galleries could be related to clusters and others are more
general, spanning several clusters. With respect to duration
it is proposed that interdisciplinary galleries whether cluster
oriented or general can be defined as short-term (in which
exhibits last 3-6 months), medium-term (in which exhibits are
planned for 3 to 5 years), or long-term (in which exhibits are
considered as "permanent").

As stated in the *Opportunities and Constraints* report, there
will be a major museum-wide temporary (short-term) exhibition
hall. The ECTF now propose that additional short-term exhibit
spaces be distributed throughout the Museum in a way that relates
to clusters. These are intended to accommodate smaller temporary exhibits whether internally generated or from outside
the Museum. In addition, there may be some departmental short-
term galleries for temporary exhibits as requested by departments for their own collections.

The proposal to provide some galleries or exhibits of medium duration deserves some explanation. These spaces are intended to accommodate interdisciplinary concepts which warrant longer exposure than in the temporary exhibits, but are not essential to the permanent statement of the Museum. Thus, complex interdisciplinary ideas can be developed which merit the effort to produce an exhibit which will last a few years. Such galleries could be either cluster-oriented or museum-wide. A long list of suggestions from departments on inter-disciplinary ideas has been assembled. The medium duration will enable many of these ideas to be realized over the next several years and will also enhance the image of the Museum as "a place where things happen".

An added advantage of this type of gallery space is that it provides a built-in flexibility to accommodate change over the years. Areas have been identified, e.g., physical anthropology, which are not now represented in the Museum and for which, some time in the future, space may be required. The designation of some spaces for medium-term exhibitions provides one means of planning for such an eventuality enabling future permanent displays to be accommodated when necessary.

The third type of multi-disciplinary gallery is space to accommodate permanently the introduction to a cluster of departmental galleries. Such space will be allocated where clusters of departments identify this as a need, or where the need emerges from discussions between the ECTF and departments.

Ideas for interdisciplinary galleries are being developed and will be presented to the curatorial departments within the next several weeks. There will be a chart developed at that time which includes such proposed galleries and their relationships to the clusters of departmental galleries.

In January we will be meeting with groups of departments identified as clusters to explore these ideas further. In the meantime we welcome your responses individually.

Thank you again for your cooperation.

E C T F   BULLETIN # 6

Interrelationships Diagrams
for Art and Archaeology, and
Sciences are found following p.18
Figures 1 and 2

E.C.T.F. BULLETIN

ROM

EXHIBITS COMMUNICATIONS TASK FORCE

NO. 7

J. Di Profio; Chairman

L. Levine; Vice Chairman

Date: February 13, 1978

INTRODUCTION

The ECTF has now reached a critical stage in the process of developing an overall plan for galleries, and would like your comments before proceeding to a final decision. We have looked at a variety of options for arranging galleries by clusters and we are presenting two of these (Plan A and Plan B) for your review. Although the ECTF strongly favours Plan A, we feel that you will be more prepared to provide us with positive criticisms, suggestions or alternatives if you are aware of both the final options considered by the ECTF, together with the rationale for their development and the advantages and disadvantages of each.

Once agreement has been reached on the arrangement of clusters and the relative amounts of space to be allocated to them, the next stage of the work of the ECTF will entail working with the departments to allocate space within their designated cluster and to allocate such shared spaces as are desired.

Please keep in mind that at this stage we are working towards a general concept. Of necessity, there are loose ends which will be worked out in detailed planning.

We are scheduled to decide upon a general gallery plan by Friday, February 24th. In effect we must decide upon Plan A or Plan B, some variation of these, or another plan entirely. Between now and February 24th, we will be arranging meetings with groups of departments according to cluster grouping in order to obtain your comments directly. To enable as many people as possible to participate in this type of forum, it would be helpful if all the curators in the various departments could attend these meetings.

We also welcome individual comments from the Museum at large. To allow sufficient time to consider all comments, we would ask that any individual comments be received in writing in the ECTF office by Tuesday, February 21st.

CLUSTERS

We are attempting to provide an arrangement of galleries which makes possible the linkages suggested by departments. This also makes possible an arrangement which is orderly and comprehensible to the Museum visitor. One obvious way of accomplishing these linkages is to arrange galleries so that those with strong conceptual ties are closely related physically. Our last bulletin proposed the concept of clusters of related galleries. This concept is reflected in both proposed plans.

Some minor adjustments have been made to the clusters as outlined in our last bulletim. The current departmental composition of the clusters is as follows:

Life Sciences:

> Botany
> Entomology
> Invertebrate Zoology
> Ichthyology and Herpetology
> Mammalogy
> Ornithology

Palaeontological
Sciences:

> Invertebrate Palaeontology
> Vertebrate Palaeontology

Earth Sciences:

> Mineralogy
> Geology

New World:

> New World Archaeology (North, Central
>   and South American)
> Ethnology*

Europe/Canada:

> European
> Canadiana (two galleries in the main
>   building)
> Textiles**
> Philately

---

*Ethnology collections not related to the New World are not included above as they do not relate strongly to any of the clusters. They will, of course, be allocated space at the stage of detailed departmental allocations.

**You will note that the Textile Department is included with several clusters. As requested by the Textile Department, its galleries will be distributed among the clusters as shown above.

Mediterranean Basin:	Greek and Roman (including European Archaeology)
	Egypt
	West Asian
	Textiles**
Far East:	Far East
	Textiles**

SPACE

The total amount of gallery space that will be available in the renovated Museum and new terrace galleries is approximately 200,000 square feet.* This is roughly 50,000 square feet more than is currently available. Clearly we are working with a limited amount of space. Most departments have requested additional space, while there are some departments which currently do not have any gallery space. In addition, there is considerable demand for non-departmental exhibit space.

The ECTF has worked with the Project Office to ensure that there will be as much usable gallery space as possible, and has tried to be as equitable as possible in allocating the available space between clusters. Both the substance of departmental gallery proposals and the actual area requests formed the basis for judgments.

At this stage we are working with space allocation by cluster. The following table indicates the amount of space requested, and the allocations in both Plan A and Plan B by cluster. It should be noted that the figures for space requested do not reflect any non-departmental gallery space, whereas the allocations do.

The space allocated for each cluster is intended to accommodate all of the departmental galleries of those departments represented in a cluster. In addition, space will be allocated within clusters for introductory galleries, short-term temporary exhibits, and medium-term (3-5 years duration) exhibits. The amount of such space in relation to departmental galleries is to be worked out in conjunction with

---

*An additional 14,000 square feet of space will be available for certain types of display on the main floor of the atrium areas. These are indicated on the floor plans as display areas.

**You will note that the Textile Department is included with several clusters. As requested by the Textile Department, its galleries will be distributed among the clusters as shown above.

the departments concerned in the next stage of our work.

There will also be some galleries which are not directly
related to the clusters. These museum-wide galleries include
Exhibition Hall, the Discovery Galleries, and space for
introduction/orientation to the Museum. It should be noted
that, when decisions were made regarding allocation of space
to various uses, museum-wide spaces were constrained with
greater emphasis being given to departmental and cluster-
related spaces.

When examining the proposed space allocations and gallery
arrangements, it should be kept in mind that the galleries
as they currently exist will be completely dismantled as
part of the renovation process. This will include the
demolition of existing walls within the Museum. In other
words, there will be opportunity for completely altering
the configuration of galleries and for making more effective
and efficient use of space than current room division makes
possible.

CLUSTER	DEPARTMENTAL REQUESTS[1]			EXIS-TING[2]	CLUSTER ALLOCATION	
	Min.	Med.	Max.		PLAN A	PLAN B
	Sq.Ft.	Sq.Ft.	Sq.Ft.	Sq.Ft.	Sq.Ft.	Sq.Ft.
Far East	27700	29000	29800	26800	24400	24400
Ming Tomb					4600	4600
Atrium					2000	2000
Mediterranean Basin	34000	39100	45600	23300	36400	35700[3]
Europe/Canada	38000	42900	46700	31600	35100	35000
New World	12300	15500	24100	12500	15000	15000
Atrium					5400	5400
Life Sciences	37200	51600	67300	18600	41000	41700
Palaeontology	18300	20300	24100	10000	16100	16100
Earth Sciences	14100	17400	19300	13800	15000	13000
Other: Exhibition Hall	10000	10000	10000	6500	9100	9100
Discovery Group	4100	6200	9000	1600	4000	4000
Introduction/ Orientation					2000	2000
TOTALS	195700	232000	275900	144700	198100	198600[4]
Ming Tomb					4600	4600
Atria					7400	7400

---

[1] As all departments did not provide a complete minimum-maximum range of figures, extrapolations were made where necessary for analysis. All figures have been rounded to the nearest hundred.

[2] Existing gallery area figures were obtained from Project Office documents, based on information gathered in 1975.

[3] An additional 2,600 sq.ft. on this floor have not yet been assigned.

[4] The difference between the Plan A and Plan B totals is due to the rounding of the area figures.

ARRANGEMENT OF GALLERIES: OBJECTIVES FOR AN OVERALL PLAN

Many factors have had to be considered in developing the arrangement of clusters. The development of a plan is a complex matter
under any circumstances. If the amount of space were adequate,
and if the building were a simple rectangle on one floor, then
the desired relationships could probably be easily accommodated.
However, there is not enough space. In addition, the building
is a complex shape with gallery areas subdivided by stairs and
escalators. Each floor has only so much area, which in some
instances precludes a logical arrangement of all closely related
departments. For example, all of the Sciences cannot be arrayed
on one floor even though it would appear to be conceptually
desirable to do so.

Some of the major objectives considered by the ECTF for developing the two proposed plans are listed below for your information:

- *To allocate the available space in a way which will ensure
  that museum-wide, cluster-related, and departmental needs
  are reasonably met.*

- *To develop a plan which will be more comprehensible to the
  visitor, and which will reflect conceptual relationships
  requested by departments.*

  As we have noted, the cluster concept will not only permit
  departments to make logical connections in their galleries,
  but should also provide basic conceptual orientation for
  the visitor. Orientation can be further reinforced by
  physically locating clusters close to one another where
  conceptual ties are the strongest. For example, locating
  the European and Mediteranean Basin clusters on the same
  floor reinforces known connections.

  The placement of clusters by floor was deliberate. Research
  conducted for the ECTF has shown that visitors do not make
  vertical connections easily. Therefore, the ECTF has
  attempted to locate complete clusters on one floor, and
  where possible, strongly linked clusters on the same floor.

- *To provide for the conservation of the collections on display.*

  Although the climate of the whole Museum will be considerably
  enhanced, the best climate controls will be available in the
  Terrace Galleries. Therefore, there has been an attempt to
  place the most sensitive collections wherever possible in the
  Terrace Galleries.

● *To reflect major constraints of existing displays.*

It was decided to accept that the existing Vertebrate
Palaeontology Gallery, the Chinese Wall-paintings and
the proposed location for the Ming Tomb will not be
changed. All other galleries are being treated as
re-locatable.

● *To best distribute the available human and financial
resources of the Museum for a 1982 opening.*

Only the Terrace Galleries and centre block portions of
the Museum are scheduled to be open to the public for
1982. Galleries that are to be developed in these two
sections of the Museum will deeply affect the workloads
of the curatorial departments concerned. Depending on
the nature of these galleries, the workload of the Exhibit
Design Services Department could also be affected dramatically. In addition, the financial resources available
to complete this first phase of the gallery plan should
be distributed in a reasonable manner.

● *To make a representative set of galleries available to the
public upon the completion of the first phase of gallery
development (January, 1982).*

Without compromising a comprehensible overall plan, it is
important that the galleries located in the terrace and
centre block areas present to the public as broad a range
as possible of the Museum's collections.

A DESCRIPTION OF PLANS A AND B

In order to assist you in assessing the two plans, and
to encourage your suggestions, we would like to describe and
review some of the factors that were considered in evolving
these plans.

Description By Floor

The First Floor: Plans A and B propose an identical first
floor, accommodating Exhibition Hall, the Far East cluster,
the New World cluster, and space for Orientation/Introduction
to the Museum.

The Second Floor: The second floor in Plan A is entirely
devoted to the Life Sciences and Palaeontological Sciences.
In Plan B only the east wing is devoted to the Sciences, and
the remainder of the floor is allocated to the Mediterranean
Basin cluster.

The Third Floor: The third floor in Plan A accommodates the
Mediterranean Basin cluster and the bulk of the Europe/Canada
galleries. In Plan B, this entire floor is devoted to the
Sciences with the exception of the Terrace Gallery, which is
allocated to the Europe/Canada cluster.

Level B1: In Plan A this level would accommodate some of the
Europe/Canada galleries as well as the Earth Sciences. In
Plan B, this would be entirely devoted to the Europe/Canada
cluster.

Level B2: In both plans, this would contain the Discovery
Group of galleries.

Rationale By Cluster

Orientation: A portion of the existing Armour Court is
proposed as an orientation area for the Museum. The results
of many ECTF studies emphasize again and again the need for
adequate orientation at the beginning of a Museum visit.
The existing Armour Court serves this function unintentionally to
a large extent now.

Exhibition Hall: There were three major considerations in
positioning Exhibition Hall: the amount of space required,
including "crush" space for openings; the availability of
good environmental conditions; and convenience of access
from the main entry. In the opinion of the ECTF, the first
floor of the south wing of the East Block best fulfills these
requirements if prime climate can be made available. The
Project Office is currently investigating the provision of
prime climate for this gallery. One additional consideration
was that while this space would function admirably as an
Exhibition Hall, its potential for a departmental gallery
is limited due to its somewhat separate location, making
conceptual connections between this and other galleries
more difficult to achieve.

Far East Cluster: The Far East collection is unquestionably
one of the finest within the ROM. The new location for the
Ming Tomb will be on the first floor at the north end of the
new Terrace Galleries. The Chinese Wall-paintings are in the

northwest wing of the first floor. Locating the Far East cluster in the northern portion of the first floor will enable this collection to be displayed in conjunction with these important elements, and at the same time will ensure that the public will have easy access to this important collection.

New World Cluster: The New World cluster contains very popular collections. The ECTF felt that it was important to give some prominence to our Native cultures. The conjunction of this cluster and the Far East cluster on the first floor will provide visitors with some indication of the strength of the ROM's collections in their very first contact with the exhibits.

Display Areas (Main Floor): The main floor areas of the atria provide some additional opportunities for display. The south-east display area could accommodate a variety of museum-wide introductory displays, and could also serve as an overflow area for Exhibition Hall when exhibitions require more than the available space within the Hall. In addition, this area will provide convenient "crush" space for exhibit openings. The northeast atrium could also serve as a museum-wide general display area. The atrium areas next to the west wing will be devoted to the New World and Far East clusters.

Science Cluster: The Vertebrate Palaeontology galleries, which have been recently completed, cannot be relocated without completely rebuilding them. Fortunately, they were built in a way which will enable the new building services to be provided around them without disturbing these very successful displays. In both plans, these galleries will therefore remain in place.

Plan A would enable all of the Life Sciences to be displayed on the second floor in conjunction with the Palaeontology galleries. The inclusion of introductory, short-term and medium-term galleries would provide opportunities for combined displays from these closely related disciplines.

In Plan B, the third floor would include the Life and Earth Sciences, while the Palaeontological Sciences would likely remain on the second floor. This plan would permit the existing Life Sciences dioramas to remain in the east wing. Plan A would necessitate their relocation and refurbishing, which is feasible at some cost and effort.

In Plan A, the Earth Sciences are located on B1 level. This is somewhat removed from the remainder of the Sciences, but

Earth Sciences have been identified as conceptually the most self-contained of the Sciences.

<u>Europe/Canada Cluster</u>: The Europe/Canada cluster is divided in both plans between the third floor and level B1. This cluster consists of one set of galleries which must remain together to provide a coherent storyline, and other galleries which could be positioned independently of the main group of galleries.

In Plan A, the major set of galleries presenting the chronological sequences of Continental and English furniture and furnishings could be on the third floor in conjunction with the Mediterranean Basin cluster. This creates opportunities for making logical connections between these two clusters.

In Plan B, the bulk of the Europe/Canada cluster is on level B1, with some of the special collections on the third floor. In this plan, more of these sensitive collections would be in prime climate areas.

<u>Mediterranean Basin Cluster</u>: In Plan A, the Mediterranean Basin cluster is located on the third floor in the west, centre and terrace galleries. In Plan B, the west, centre and terrace galleries of the second floor are devoted to the Mediterranean Basin cluster.

In Plan A, the physical proximity and the close conceptual relationship between the Mediterranean Basin and the Europe/Canada clusters would enable short-and medium-term galleries to service both clusters conveniently. Also, galleries could be arranged to flow chronologically (from the last Greek and Roman gallery into the first chronological sequence of the Europe/Canada cluster), and to create logical connections between Mediaeval Europe and Mediaeval Islam.

<u>Discovery Group</u>: The Discovery Group of galleries is an extension of the highly successful Discovery Room. These are tentatively located on level B2 adjacent to the Education Department. These gallery spaces have low ceilings and are not suitable for traditional gallery uses.

<u>CONCLUSION</u>

After narrowing down the options to two plans, the ECTF then compared the disadvantages of each. The following summary lists were developed:

Plan A

1)   Earth Sciences are separated from the other Sciences.

2)   More of the European collection is out of prime climate gallery space.

3)   Requires moving Life Sciences dioramas.

Plan B

1)   All the Life Sciences are not together.

2)   The Europe/Canada cluster and the Mediterranean Basin cluster are not together.

3)   Life Sciences dioramas dictate the arrangement and design of galleries on the third floor.

4)   Life Sciences dioramas constrain the building renovation programme.

5)   Poor distribution of resources through to opening in January, 1982.

6)   Poor distribution of galleries available to the public at opening in January, 1982.

The ECTF strongly recommends Plan A. We feel that this plan best fulfills the objectives set out previously. This arrangement of galleries in our view provides excellent long-term opportunities for collections and ideas to be presented to the public in an effective and comprehensible way. In addition, it will provide a reasonable array of displays for the public at the completion of the first phase of gallery development, while providing for a fair distribution of the workload among the staff during that period of intense activity.

We invite your comments and suggestions to assist us in finalizing the overall general plan. When this is done, we will undertake the more detailed allocations of space within the overall plan.

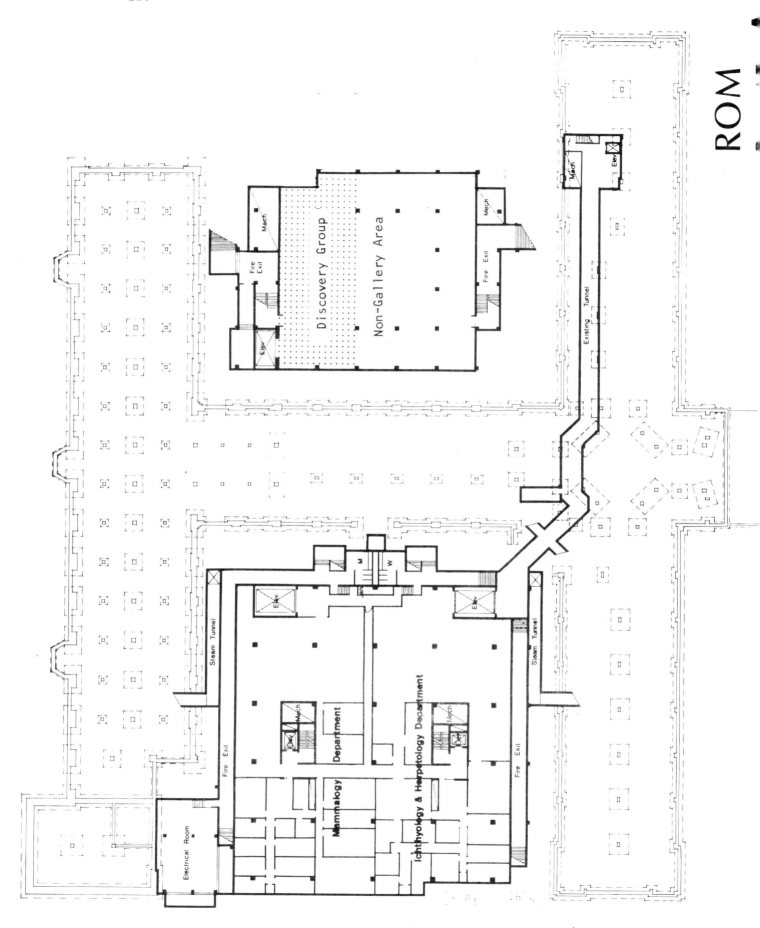

ROM

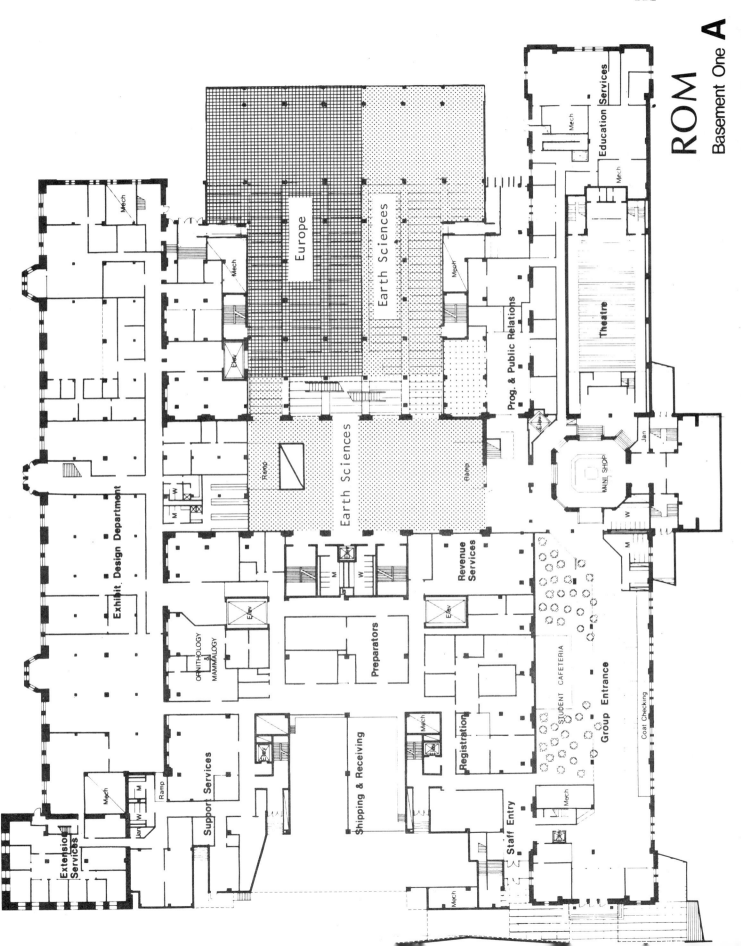

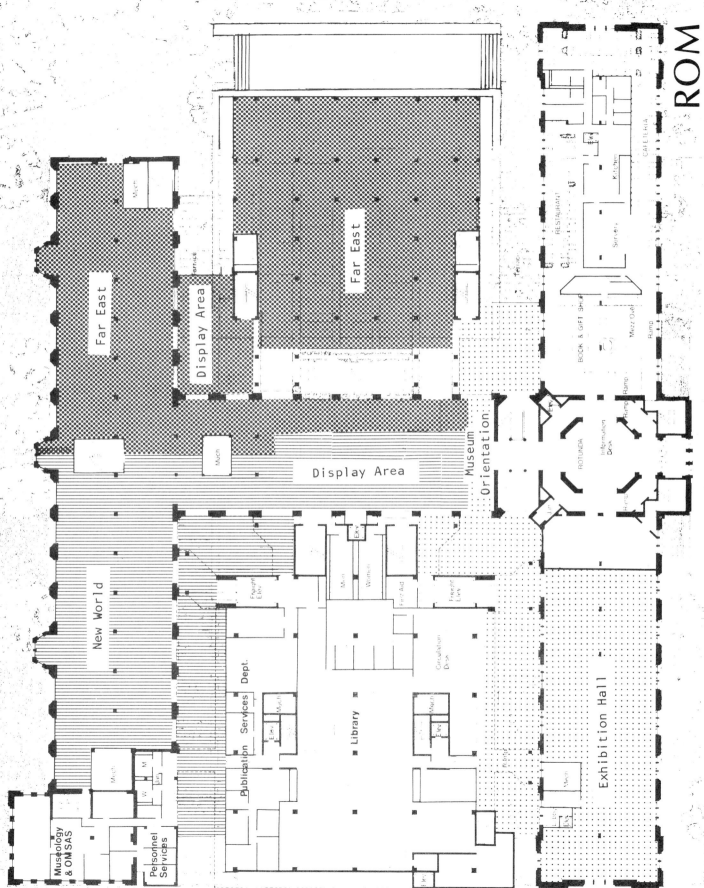

ROM
First Floor **A**

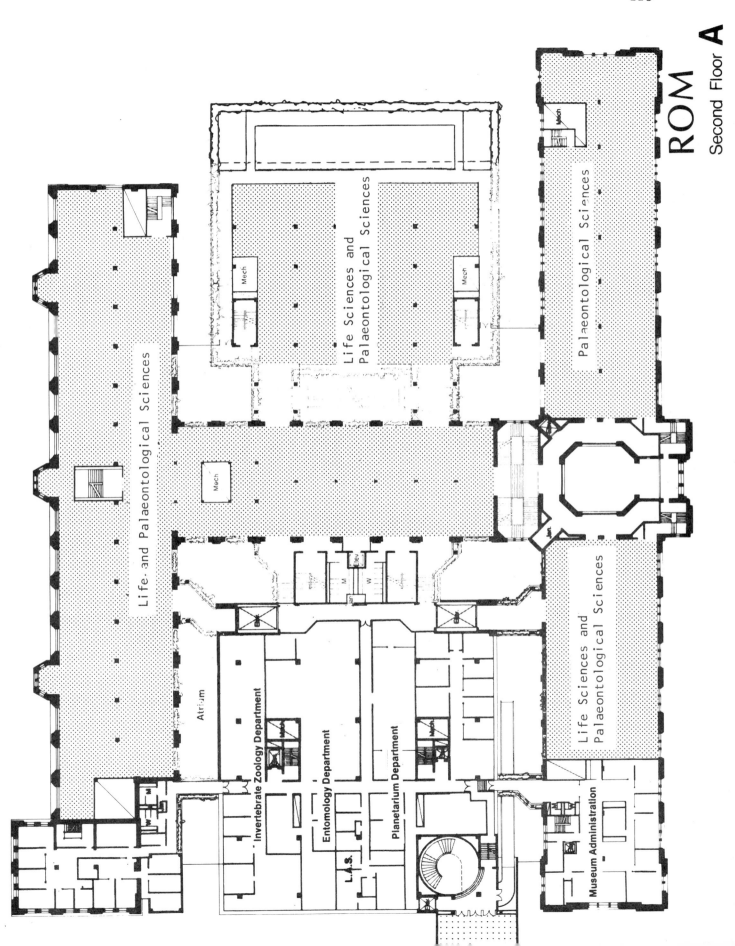

Palaeontological Sciences

Life Sciences and
Palaeontological Sciences

Life and Palaeontological Sciences

Mech

Mech

Mech

Mech

Mech

Atrium

Elev

M
W

Invertebrate Zoology Department

Entomology Department

L.A.S.

Planetarium Department

Mech

Mech

Life Sciences and
Palaeontological Sciences

Museum Administration

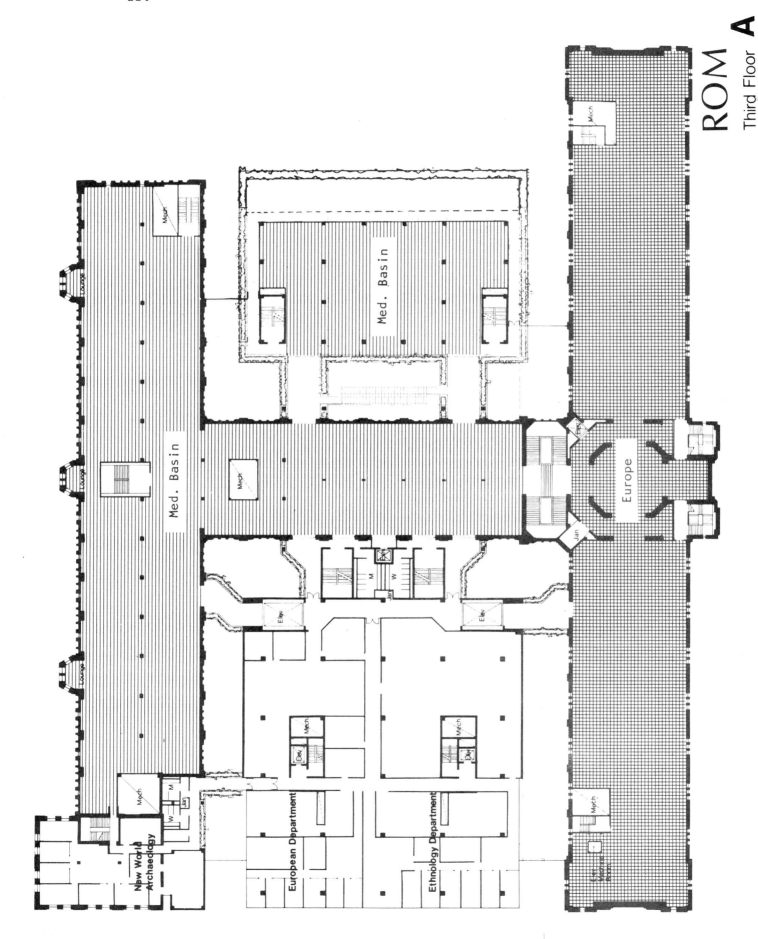

ROM **A**
Third Floor

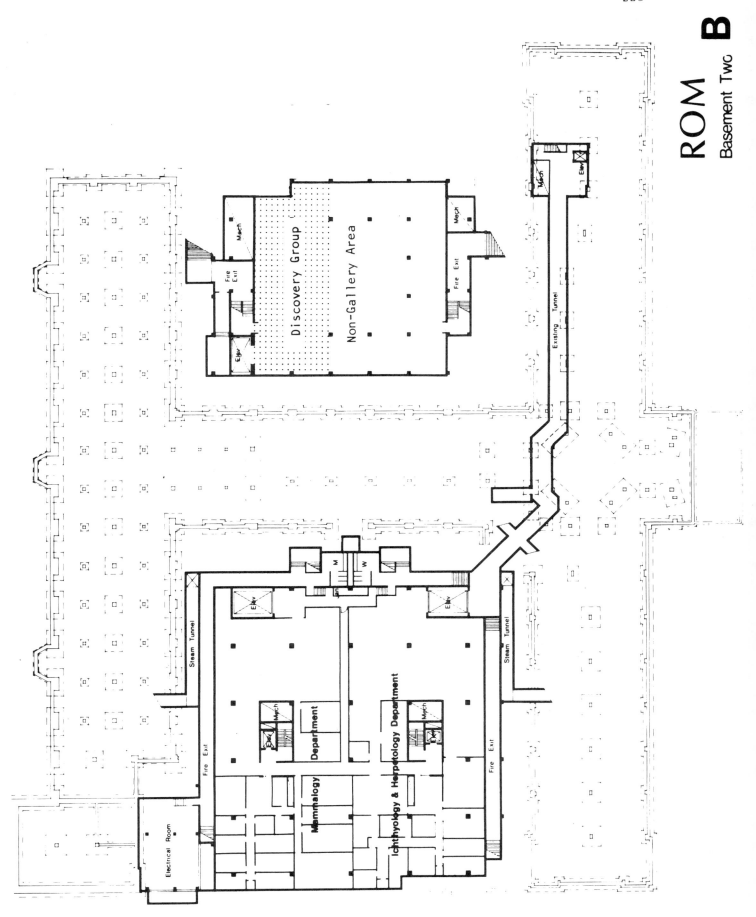

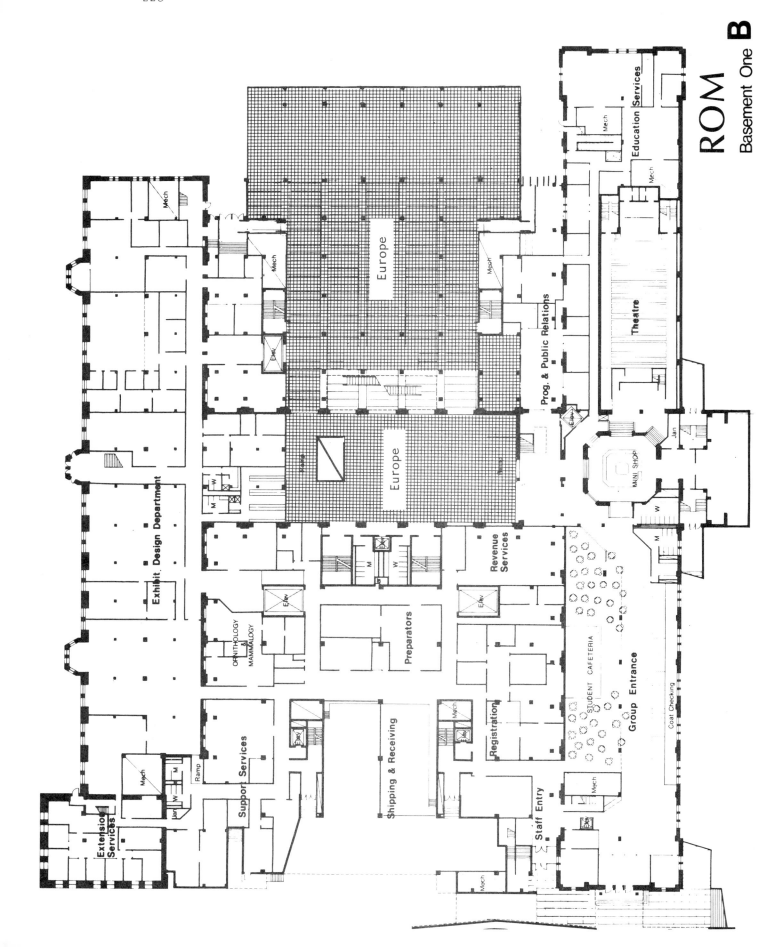

Education Services

Mech

Mech

Theatre

Europe

Mech

Prog. & Public Relations

Jan

MINI SHOP

W

M

Exhibit. Design Department

Mech

Europe

Mech

Revenue Services

M W

Preparators

ORNITHOLOGY & MAMMALOGY

Registration

Mech

STUDENT CAFETERIA

Group Entrance

Support Services

Shipping & Receiving

Ramp

M W Jan

Mech

Coat Checking

Extension Services

Staff Entry

Mech

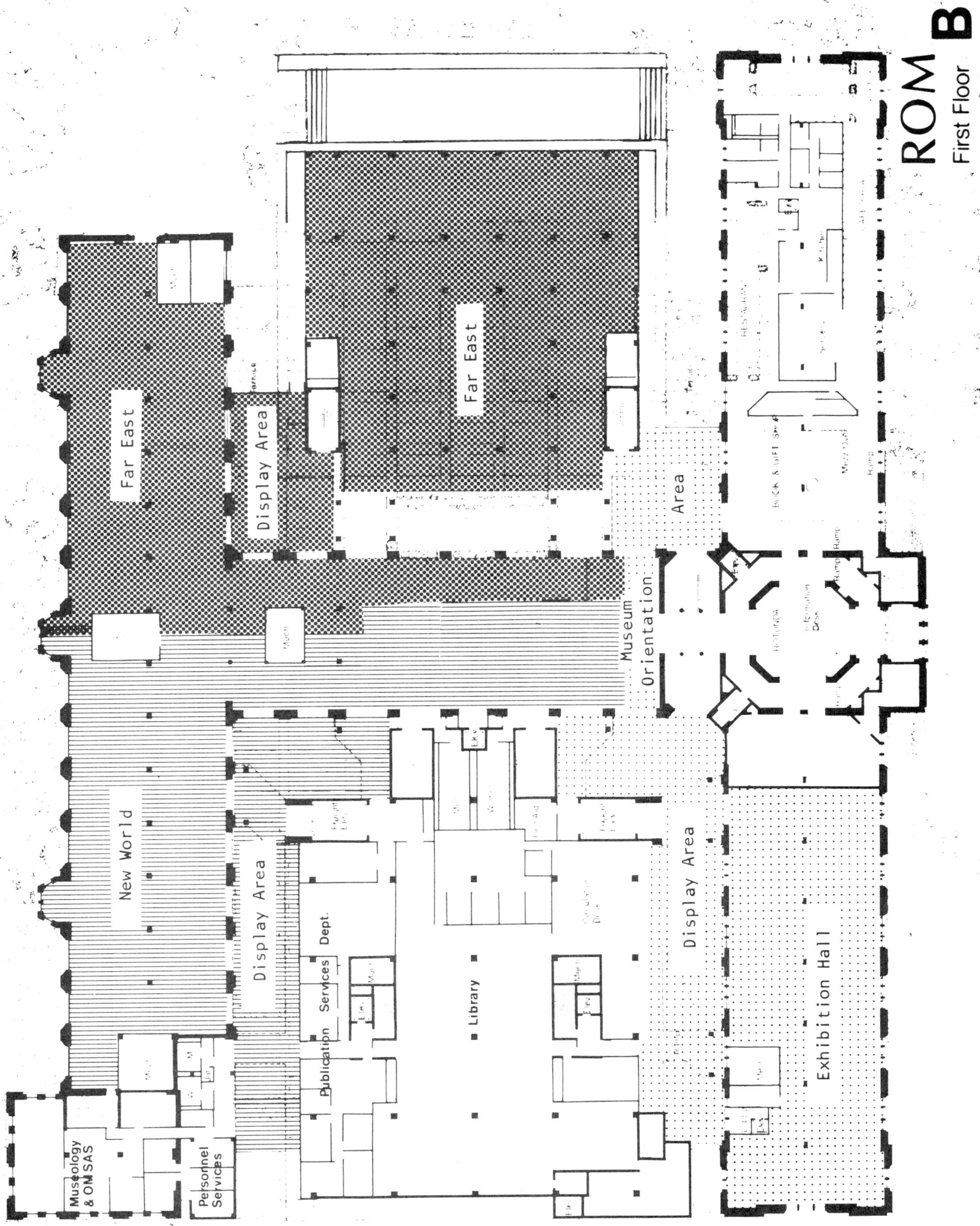

ROM B

First Floor

Far East

Far East

Display Area

Museum Orientation Area

New World

Display Area

Publication Services Dept.

Museology & OM SAS

Personnel Services

Library

Display Area

Exhibition Hall

BOOK & GIFT SHOP

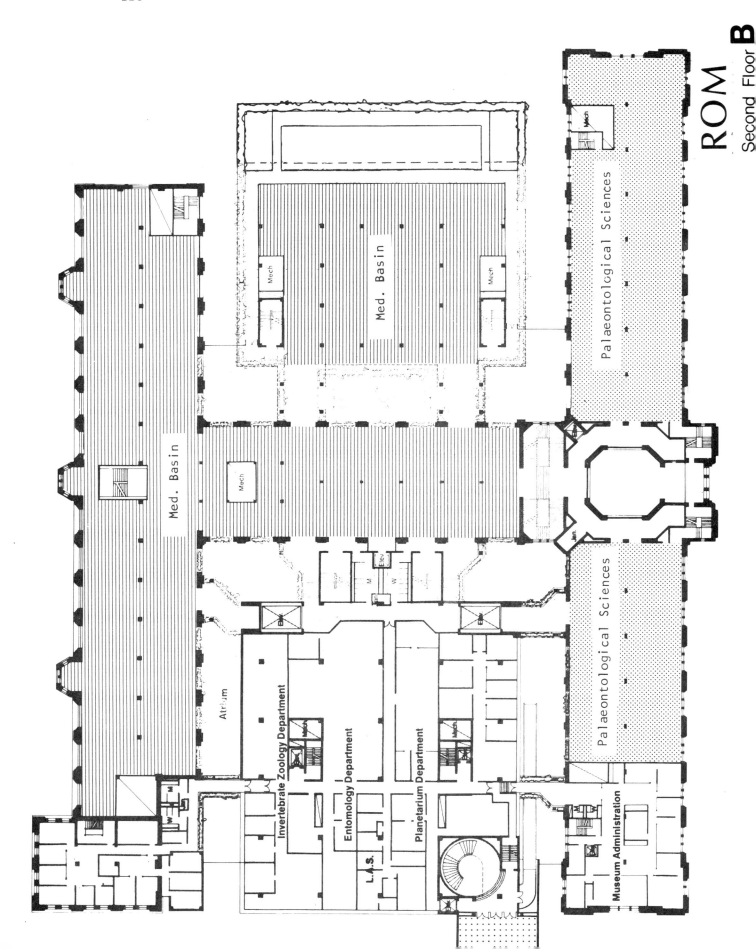

ROM **B**
Second Floor

Palaeontological Sciences

Med. Basin

Mech

Mech

Med. Basin

Mech

Palaeontological Sciences

Atrium

Invertebrate Zoology Department

Entomology Department

L.A.S.

Planetarium Department

Museum Administration

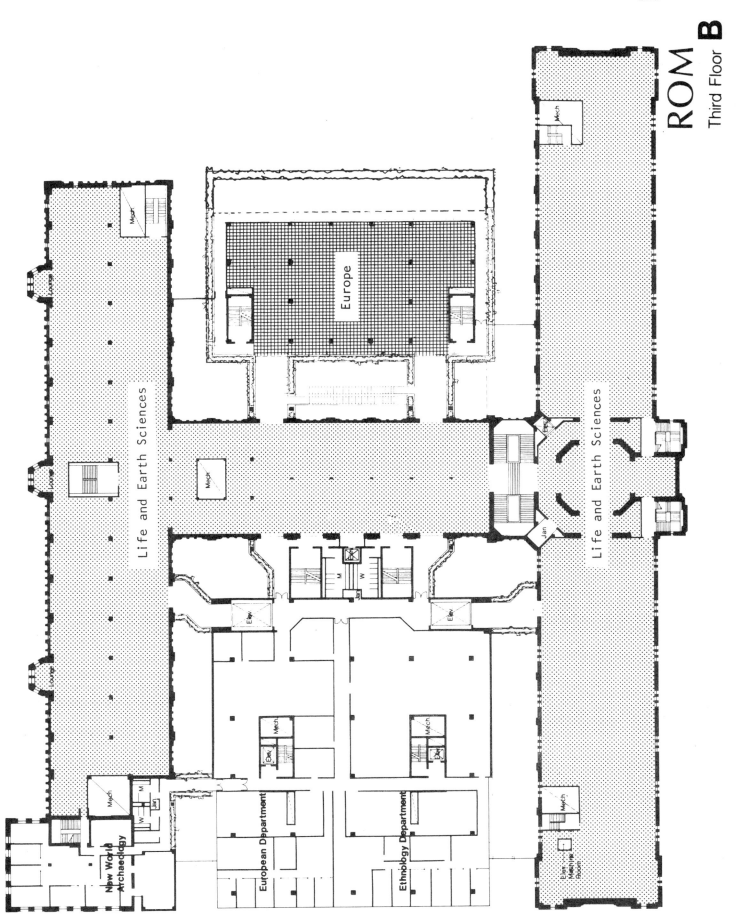

New World
Archaeology

European Department

Ethnology Department

Life and Earth Sciences

Life and Earth Sciences

Europe

Appendix C: Summary Description of Survey and Evaluation Activities

SUMMARY DESCRIPTION OF SURVEY AND EVALUATION ACTIVITIES

The following is a summary of the evaluation programme undertaken by the ECTF at the ROM during 1977.

VISITOR PERCEPTION AND PROFILE SURVEY (VPP)

The VPP was a comprehensive study*, carefully structured and rigorously conducted in order to provide an accurate data base for planning purposes. Close to 5,000 interviews were completed over four-day periods in each month of the 1977 calendar year to provide a substantial and accurate sample of the visitor population. Every tenth visitor over five years of age who entered the ROM during the survey periods was interviewed.

The purpose of this study was two-fold

(a)   to obtain an accurate picture of who visits the
       ROM, and,

(b)   to gain some insights into how visitors perceive
       the ROM and the extent to which their perceptions
       coincide with the overall objectives of the Museum.

As a result of this study the ROM is one of the few museums in North America which can provide accurate data on its visitors and can therefore plan for an audience which can be precisely defined.

VISITOR CIRCULATION PATTERN STUDY (VCP)

The Visitor Circulation Pattern Study was undertaken to identify in general terms how visitors use the Museum and the varying intensities of use at specific points throughout the ROM.

---

*Since the Canadiana Galleries of the ROM are located separately
 from the ROM's main building, a supplementary survey was conducted
 at the Canadiana Building.

Two methods of evaluation were employed: floor counts and
tracking observations. The first consisted of counting the
number of visitors who passed various locations within the
Museum. In addition to the count, demographic data were
ascertained by observation for every twentieth visitor to
pass each position. These counts were conducted over six
weekdays and six weekend days over three months. During
the same periods, some tracking observations were undertaken to identify general circulation patterns and problems.
This involved following visitors throughout their visit to
the ROM from entry to exit. Supplementary observations were
made in areas which had been identified as having particular
circulation problems. This occurred over four days of the
March school break.

OVERALL VISITOR TRACKING AND SATISFACTION SURVEY (OVTSS)

The OVTSS was undertaken as an extensive survey of visitors'
reactions to the entire Museum. The purpose of this survey
was to examine in detail the way in which the Museum as a
whole is used by its visitors and the overall satisfaction
with which they regard their visits. One in every forty
persons over twelve years of age was tracked for the duration
of his visit to the Museum and then interviewed. A total of
222 tracking observations and 178 questionnaires were completed during six days in August and November, including
weekdays and weekends.

Supplementary to the OVTSS, tracking observations were
undertaken in the Rotunda to discover how casual visitors
use the Rotunda both with the turnstiles in place and after
the renovations and installation of the new information desk.
Every twentieth casual visitor was tracked from his entry by
the front doors and passage through the Rotunda until the
visitor either changed floors or entered a gallery or service
area. A total of 164 observations were completed during
several of the days on which the OVTSS was also conducted.

DISCOVERY ROOM EVALUATION (DRE)

The ECTF decided early in its deliberations to establish and
test the appropriateness of the "Discovery Room" concept for
inclusion in an overall plan. A Working Group of the ECTF,
with broad curatorial representation, was set up to investigate the concept and to subsequently plan and develop a

discovery room. Staff assistance was provided from the outset
to assist in defining objectives and in designing and carrying
out an evaluation programme to test those objectives.

The purpose of the evaluation was both to provide an overall
assessment of the success of the Room and to assist the
Working Group in developing new components and re-designing
or adjusting existing components. While a detailed evaluation
based on the objectives of individual components was not undertaken, the evaluation provides some indication of which components are working and which are not.

One in every eight persons, over nine years of age, who
entered the Discovery Room was tracked for the duration of
his visit of the Room and then interviewed. A total of 193
tracking observations were undertaken and 131 questionnaires
were administered. This survey was conducted for five days
in August and seven days in December. Both weekends and weekdays were included.

INDIVIDUAL GALLERY EVALUATIONS (IGE)

The ECTF decided to evaluate eleven existing galleries which
reflected considerable differences in subject matter, age
of gallery, design, location in the Museum, and approaches
to didactic information. The galleries evaluated were:
Textiles, Ontario Prehistory, Egyptian, Islamic Arts, Early
and Han China, Sung and Yuan Ceramics, Mineralogy, Invertebrate
Fossils, Vertebrate Fossils, Canadian Fish, and the Planetarium
display area.

The purpose of this evaluation programme was to determine the
effectiveness of the galleries by examining both the way in
which each gallery is used by visitors and to obtain visitors'
reactions to their visits. This examination of existing
galleries was designed to assist in the planning of new
galleries by indicating how well existing galleries do,
in fact, work.

The samples obtained ranged from 65 tracking observations in
the Islamic Arts Galleries to 212 in the Egyptian Galleries.
Every fifth person (every tenth in the Mineralogy and Vertebrate Fossils Galleries) over twelve years of age was tracked
for the duration of his visit and then interviewed. This
survey was conducted during a total of six days in both

August and October, except for the Planetarium display area and Invertebrate Fossils Gallery which were evaluated for the same amount of time in November.

DRAGON THRONE EVALUATION (DTE)

The purpose of this study was to evaluate the effectiveness of the temporary exhibit, "In The Presence Of The Dragon Throne", from the visitor's point of view and in terms of the objectives set by Museum staff.

The overall curatorial objectives in developing this exhibit were to inform the visitor about Chinese culture and very simply to show part of the Textile Department's collection. More specifically, the purpose of the exhibit was to convey the political importance of clothing in China. As part of this evaluation, various aspects of the display such as lighting, didactic information, spatial organization and complementary exhibits were considered in terms of the effectiveness of each in creating an exhibit which met the objectives.

The Programmes and Public Relations Department undertook a very specific publicity programme for this show. Another function of the evaluation was to help assess the effectiveness of that programme.

One in every ten persons over twelve years of age was approached upon leaving the exhibit and asked to respond to a questionnaire. One in every twenty persons, over twelve years of age, who entered the exhibit was tracked for the duration of his visit. The results are based on 234 questionnaires and 81 tracking observations. Interviews were conducted during four full days and tracking during three full days in June and July. Both weekdays and weekends were selected.

CURRENT RESEARCH CASE EVALUATION (RC)

There is a great deal of interest within the various curatorial departments of the ROM in communicating more about their research to the public. The ECTF decided that it would be useful to have some sense of visitor interest in research and to test the effectiveness of presenting this kind of information in a display.

A research case to accommodate temporary displays on current departmental research was put in place September, 1977. This study examined the first two displays to be installed in this case: the first by the West Asian Department, and the second by the Vertebrate Palaeontology Department.

The purpose of this study was two-fold: to determine to what extent ROM visitors are interested in research; and to determine the effectiveness of the individual displays in communicating with the visitor.

A total of 31 interviews were conducted for the first presentation and 36 were conducted during the second. Every fifth person to stop at the case was interviewed during a period of several days.

EUROPEAN GALLERIES OBSERVATION

The European Department conveyed a concern to the ECTF that artifacts in the galleries were being damaged because visitors were handling the unprotected furniture. The ECTF decided to use the European Galleries as a test case to assess the extent and causes of the security problems and then to test various proposed solutions. (Note: the latter part of this study was not undertaken.) After initial general observations, two periods of formal observation were undertaken. The first consisted of three hours of structured observation and the second consisted of tracking visitors and filling out a "record of contact" form for each visitor who touched an object in any way.

TRACKING OF MEMBERS' TOURS (TMT)

Both the nature and amount of orientation information provided for visitors are important aspects affecting how they use the Museum. As the Members' Committee of the ROM expressed an interest in examining the effectiveness of their tour pro-gramme, the ECTF undertook this study of the tours with the following overall purpose in mind: to determine if tours

have an effect on visitors regarding their use of the rest
of the Museum, i..e., improving physical and conceptual
orientation within individual galleries, and within the
ROM as a whole.

Two survey methods were used to evaluate the effects of
the Members' Tours. The purpose of the first method was
to obtain detailed information on visitors' reactions to
the tours. It consisted of tracking a selected sample of
visitors both during and after the tour and the administration of a questionnaire. A total of 16 tracking observations and questionnaires were completed during six days
in June.

The second method was intended to obtain more general
information on visitors' reactions over a longer period.
From July to October tour guides were asked to distribute
card questionnaires to all visitors on each tour and to
request that visitors complete the cards after the tour
and deposit them in a box provided at the information desk.
A total of 52 completed cards were collected.

Appendix D: Gallery Proposal Form

Royal Ontario Museum

To: All Curatorial Departments

From: L. Levine,
Vice-Chairman, ECTF

Subject: Gallery Request Form

Memorandum:

Date: September 5, 1977

The policy statements contained in the Opportunities & Constraints Report have now been approved, and it is time to come to grips with the reality of allocating space to various galleries and locating them within the expanded Museum.

The attached form is to help you provide the ECTF with a preliminary statement of your ideas and requirements for galleries. This form consists of eight parts. The first five are specific to your departmental galleries and must be answered. Parts six to eight refer to other galleries and issues, and we would like your opinions on them.

One of the problems that we had in designing this form was that departmental collections are dramatically different in size and scale, with some departments encompassing more than one collection. In addition, the approach to displaying collections varies from department to department. As a result, it was hard to find a word to cover many situations which exist or which could appear. For example, the mineralogy display is now in a single space with a number of components, while the Far Eastern and Ethnology collections are spread into a number of spaces. In the end, we returned to the familiar "gallery" as the operative term, but we have set up a number of categories to further define this term. We would like to know which category your department intends to use, regardless of current circumstances.

The categories are:

1) A single "gallery".

2) A series of "galleries" all very closely related, both conceptually and physically, in a sequence.

3) A series of relatively independent "galleries" with some conceptual or physical connections.

4) A series of independent "galleries" with no significant physical or conceptual connections.

5) Other, please describe.

The word "gallery" in all of these options has no maximum space component. It can be 2,000, 3,000 or even 10,000 square feet. However, for present purposes a gallery should be considered as no less than approximately 1,000 square feet. (For scale, the area of the Bronze Age Far Eastern Gallery is about 1,200 square feet.)

In order to help us process this mass of material, a consistent
set of questions is being posed to all departments. If more than
one gallery is proposed, a separate Part 2 is necessary for each
gallery. Extra copies of Part 2 are available from the ECTF
office.

If you find this form in any way inadequate for your requirements,
please feel free to attach additional comments. Any questions
regarding the forms can be addressed to me or to Henry Sears or
Betty Kaser at Ext. 5429.

We would like these forms returned as soon as possible, and at
the latest by the end of the month. Shortly thereafter we will
be interviewing all departments to clarify or expand upon the
points raised in this questionnaire.

Royal Ontario Museum
Exhibits Communication Task Force
Gallery Proposal Form

Department: _243_ _____

Completed by: _____

Date: _____

Part 1 **Overall Gallery Proposal**

---

*The following questions should be answered in the most general
overall terms. Detailed descriptions of individual components
form Part 2. of this proposal format.*

a) COLLECTION(S)

   Describe briefly the features, quantity and quality
   of your collection(s) and as well those aspects of
   the work of your department that you feel the
   public would be interested in.

   _____

   _____

   _____

   _____

   _____

   _____

   _____

   _____

   _____

   _____

b) OVERALL PURPOSE OF "GALLERY"

   Provide a brief overall statement of purpose for
   what you would like to present to the public in
   your gallery(ies).

   _____

   _____

   _____

   _____

   _____

   _____

   _____

   _____

   _____

   _____

c) <u>ORGANIZATION OF GALLERY SPACE</u>

Indicate which of the following illustrates how you would organize your collection(s) spatially to fulfill the purpose you have described above.

1) A single "gallery".

2) A series of "galleries" all very closely related both conceptually and physically in a sequence.

3) A series of relatively independent "galleries" with some physical or conceptual connections.

4) A series of independent "galleries" with no significant physical or conceptual connections.

5) Other, please describe.

If your overall organization is anything other than Option 1, please list or briefly describe the galleries and describe the relationships between them. (e.g. is the organization chronological, geographic, thematic, systematic, etc?)

Gallery 1: _____
_____

Gallery 2: _____
_____

Gallery 3: _____
_____

Gallery 4: _____
_____

Gallery 5: _____
_____

Gallery 6: _____
_____

Gallery 7: _____
_____

Gallery 8: _____
_____

Gallery 9: _____
_____

Gallery 10: _____
_____

d) OVERALL DESIGN

*The following questions are directed to the overall concept
or set of galleries. Individual gallery design concerns
should be addressed in Part 2.*

- Describe features of your collection which serve
  as focal points within your gallery(ies) or
  within the museum.

_____

_____

_____

_____

_____

_____

_____

- Describe the overall atmosphere that you would
  like to create for your gallery(ies).

_____

_____

_____

_____

_____

_____

_____

- Is the concept for your gallery(ies) one of
  changing or rotating displays, fixed displays,
  or a combination of these?

_____

_____

_____

_____

_____

_____

_____

- Describe any special spatial requirements such as
  ceiling heights (e.g. re size of objects).

_____

_____

_____

_____

_____

_____

_____

- Describe any overall conservation requirements.

_____

_____

_____

_____

_____

_____

_____

- Describe any special overall lighting requirements
  (e.g. need for natural light).

_____

_____

_____

_____

_____

_____

_____

- If there are any other aspects please feel free
  to comment.

_____

_____

_____

_____

_____

_____

_____

Part 2   **Definition of an Individual Gallery**

If your proposal is a single "gallery" approach, please complete
Part 2 once. If your proposal is an approach involving more
than one "gallery", please complete one Part 2 for each of the
"galleries" in your proposal.

a) <u>PURPOSE</u>   *(omit if proposal is a single gallery)*

    Provide a statement of purpose for what you will
present to the public in this gallery.

_____

_____

_____

_____

_____

_____

_____

_____

_____

_____

b) <u>CONTENT AND ORGANIZATION</u>

    Briefly describe what the public will see in this
gallery and how it is organized.   *(This could provide*
the basis for an introductory statement on the wall of the
gallery.)

_____

_____

_____

_____

_____

_____

_____

_____

_____

_____

c) COLLECTION(S)

What artifacts/specimens will be displayed in this gallery?

_____

_____

_____

_____

_____

- To what extent will artifacts/specimens be rotated?

_____

_____

_____

_____

_____

- How would you like to see them presented? For example,
  would they be most advantageously shown in groups
  or clusters, or individually?

_____

_____

_____

_____

_____

- To what extent will new artifacts/specimens have to be
  acquired for this gallery?

_____

_____

_____

_____

_____

- Is there anything about your artifacts/specimens which
  requires complex or time consuming preparation prior
  to installation?

_____

_____

_____

_____

_____

d) SUPPORT MATERIALS

What support materials (photographs, audio-visual, context, settings, test material) would you like to include in this gallery to complement your collection and inform the visitor?

_____

_____

_____

_____

_____

_____

_____

_____

_____

_____

_____

_____

_____

e) CONSERVATION

What specific conservation requirements (humidity, light, heat, etc.) must be dealt with to properly protect this portion of your collection?

_____

_____

_____

_____

_____

_____

_____

_____

_____

_____

_____

_____

_____

f) <u>SECURITY</u>

What special security considerations must be dealt
with to protect this portion of your collection?
(particularly valuable objects/ specimens, very
fragile objects/specimens, very popular objects/
specimens).

_____

_____

_____

_____

_____

_____

_____

_____

_____

_____

_____

g) <u>DESIGN</u>

Describe any specific design issues pertaining to
this gallery which will affect spatial or
locational requirements? (e.g. dense or sparse
display, extent of didactic material, atmosphere/
dramatic effects, period settings, etc.)

_____

_____

_____

_____

_____

_____

_____

_____

_____

_____

_____

Part 3   **Estimated Gallery Areas**

a) Indicate a range* of spatial requirements for
   your gallery or set of galleries.

   Maximum: ————— sq. ft.

   Medium: ————— sq. ft.

   Minimum: ————— sq. ft.

b) How much space do you need for each of the
   individual galleries you have defined?

Galleries	Minimum	Area Medium	Maximum
1	—————	—————	—————
2	—————	—————	—————
3	—————	—————	—————
4	—————	—————	—————
5	—————	—————	—————
6	—————	—————	—————
7	—————	—————	—————
8	—————	—————	—————
9	—————	—————	—————
10	———————————————————————————		
Total Area	———————————————————————————		

* All departments currently occupying more than 5,000 square feet of
  gallery space must set their minimum scale at a figure which is
  less than the current departmental gallery space.

c) If the maximum spatial allocation were available,
   how would this affect your proposal? For example,
   would you add more components? Would you expand
   or change your concept? Would individual
   galleries have more on display?

_____
_____
_____
_____
_____
_____
_____
_____
_____
_____
_____
_____
_____
_____
_____
_____
_____
_____
_____
_____
_____
_____
_____
_____
_____
_____
_____
_____

d) If the minimum spatial allocation were available,
how would this affect your proposal? For example,
would you decrease the number of components, change
your concept, rotate more material, etc.?

_____

_____

_____

_____

_____

_____

_____

_____

_____

_____

_____

_____

_____

_____

_____

_____

_____

_____

_____

_____

_____

_____

_____

_____

_____

_____

_____

_____

_____

Part 4 **Existing Gallery(ies)**

a) Approximately how much gallery area does your
   collection currently occupy? _____ sq. ft.
   *(Answer only if this No. is specifically different from
   that given in the Opportunities & Constraints Report)*

b) How does your proposed gallery(ies) differ from
   the existing gallery(ies) in terms of approach,
   organization, space?

   _____

   _____

   _____

   _____

   _____

   _____

   _____

   _____

   _____

c) Which parts of your existing gallery are easy to
   relocate, somewhat difficult to relocate, or very
   difficult to relocate?

   *(For example the Chinese wall paintings would be difficult
   to relocate; the Athens Gallery would be difficult to
   relocate. On the other hand, the Greek Sculptures would
   be easy to relocate.)*

   _____

   _____

   _____

   _____

   _____

   _____

   _____

   _____

   _____

Part 5 **Relationship to Other Galleries**

a) Which galleries would you like to see adjacent
   or near to yours? Why?

_____

_____

_____

_____

_____

_____

_____

_____

_____

_____

_____

_____

b) Which departmental galleries are likely to have
   substantial areas of overlap with yours?
   Describe -

_____

_____

_____

_____

_____

_____

_____

_____

_____

_____

_____

_____

Part 6 **Interdisciplinary Galleries**

a) What interdisciplinary ideas would your department
   like to participate in developing into a gallery(ies)?

_____

_____

_____

_____

_____

_____

_____

b) What kind of contribution would your department
   make e.g. collections, concepts, etc.?

_____

_____

_____

_____

_____

_____

_____

c) What other interdisciplinary galleries would
   you like to see developed in the museum?

_____

_____

_____

_____

_____

_____

_____

Part 7 **General Galleries**

a) Which general galleries would your department
   like to see developed within the museum?

_____

_____

_____

_____

_____

_____

_____

_____

_____

_____

_____

_____

b) What contribution could your department make
   to such galleries?

_____

_____

_____

_____

_____

_____

_____

_____

_____

_____

Part 8 **Overall Gallery Plan**

a) Do you have any views on the overall plan for
   galleries? How should the museum galleries be
   organized (keeping in mind that there will be
   departmental, interdisciplinary and general
   galleries)? Is there an overall concept that
   you would recommend?

_____

_____

_____

_____

_____

_____

_____

_____

_____

_____

b) Do you have any comments about the location
   of your own gallery(ies) and the relationship
   to other galleries in the overall gallery
   plan?

_____

_____

_____

_____

_____

_____

_____

_____

_____

_____

Appendix E: Museums Visited by ECTF Members

MUSEUMS VISITED BY ECTF MEMBERS

The following is a list of the museums at which ECTF members interviewed staff, visited and photographed galleries during 1976 and 1977:

American Museum of Natural History,
New York, New York

Art Gallery of Greater Victoria,
Victoria, British Columbia

Art Institute of Chicago,
Chicago, Illinois

British Columbia Provincial Museum,
Victoria, British Columbia

Brooklyn Children's Museum,
Brooklyn, New York

Cooper-Hewitt Museum,
New York, New York

Field Museum of Natural History,
Chicago, Illinois

Florida State Museum,
Gainsville, Florida

Glenbow-Alberta Institute,
Calgary, Alberta

Manitoba Museum of Man and Nature,
Winnipeg, Manitoba

Metropolitan Museum of Art,
New York, New York

Mexican National Museum of Anthropology,
Mexico, District Federal, Mexico

Milwaukee Public Museum,
Milwaukee, Wisconsin

Museum of Anthropology,
University of British Columbia,
Vancouver, British Columbia

Oriental Institute Museum,
Chicago, Illinois

Sainte-Marie Among the Hurons,
Midland, Ontario

Smithsonian Institution,
Washington, District of Columbia
   Arts and Industry Building
   Hirshhorn Museum and Sculpture Gardens
   National Air and Space Museum
   National Museum of History and Technology
   National Museum of Natural History
   Office of Exhibits Central

Vancouver Centennial Museum,
Vancouver, British Columbia

Winnipeg Art Gallery,
Winnipeg, Manitoba.

Figure 27: Ancient World Cluster

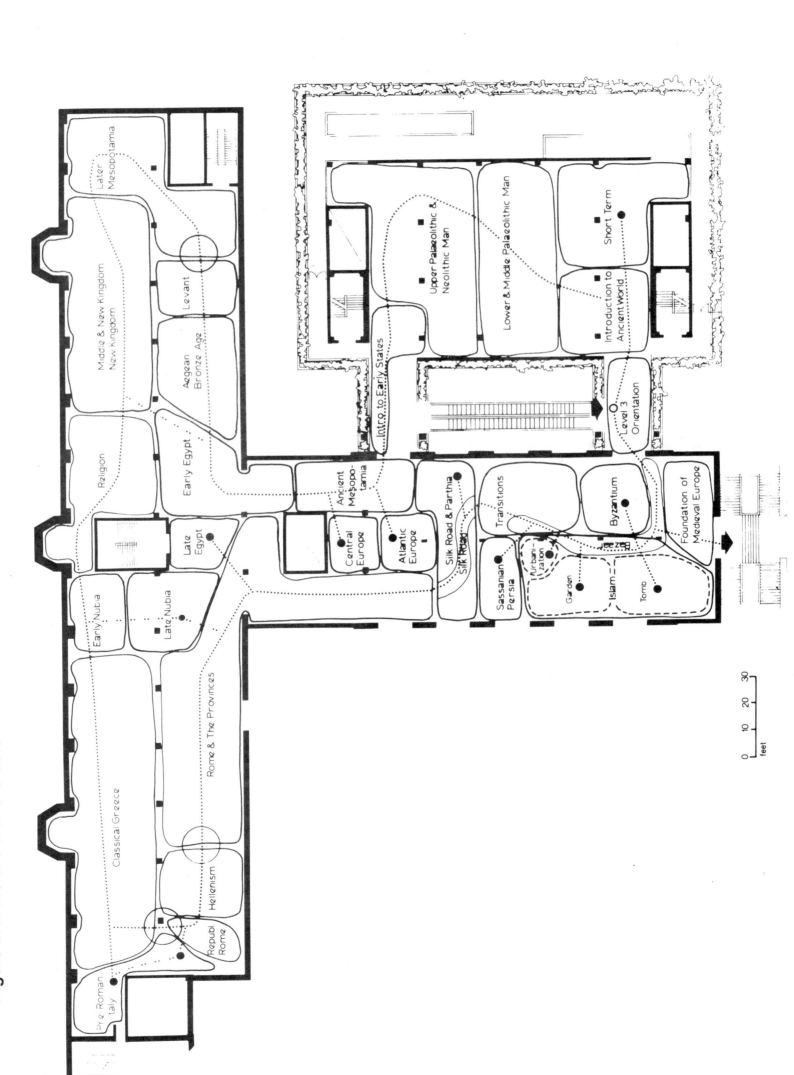

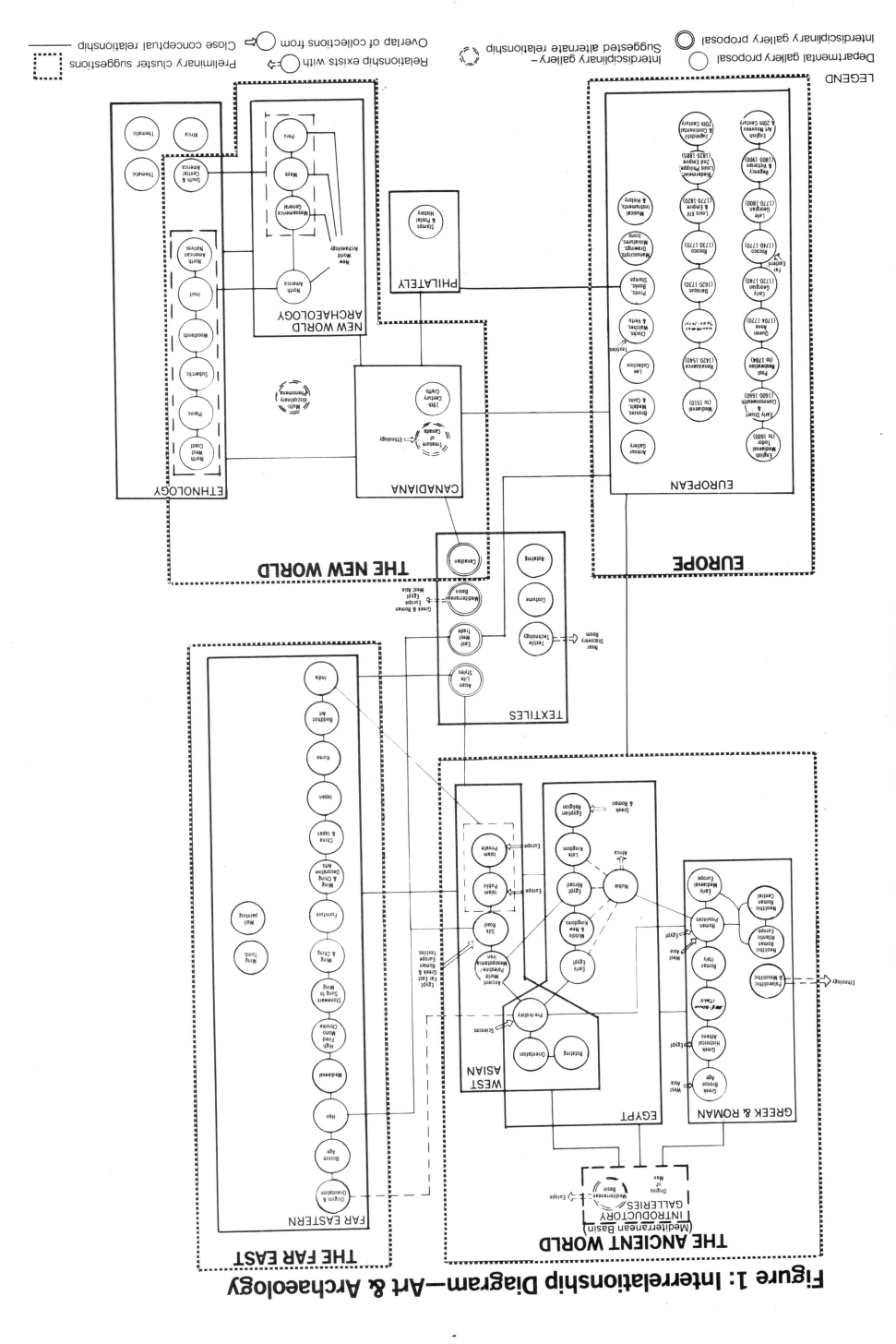

Figure 1: Interrelationship Diagram—Art & Archaeology

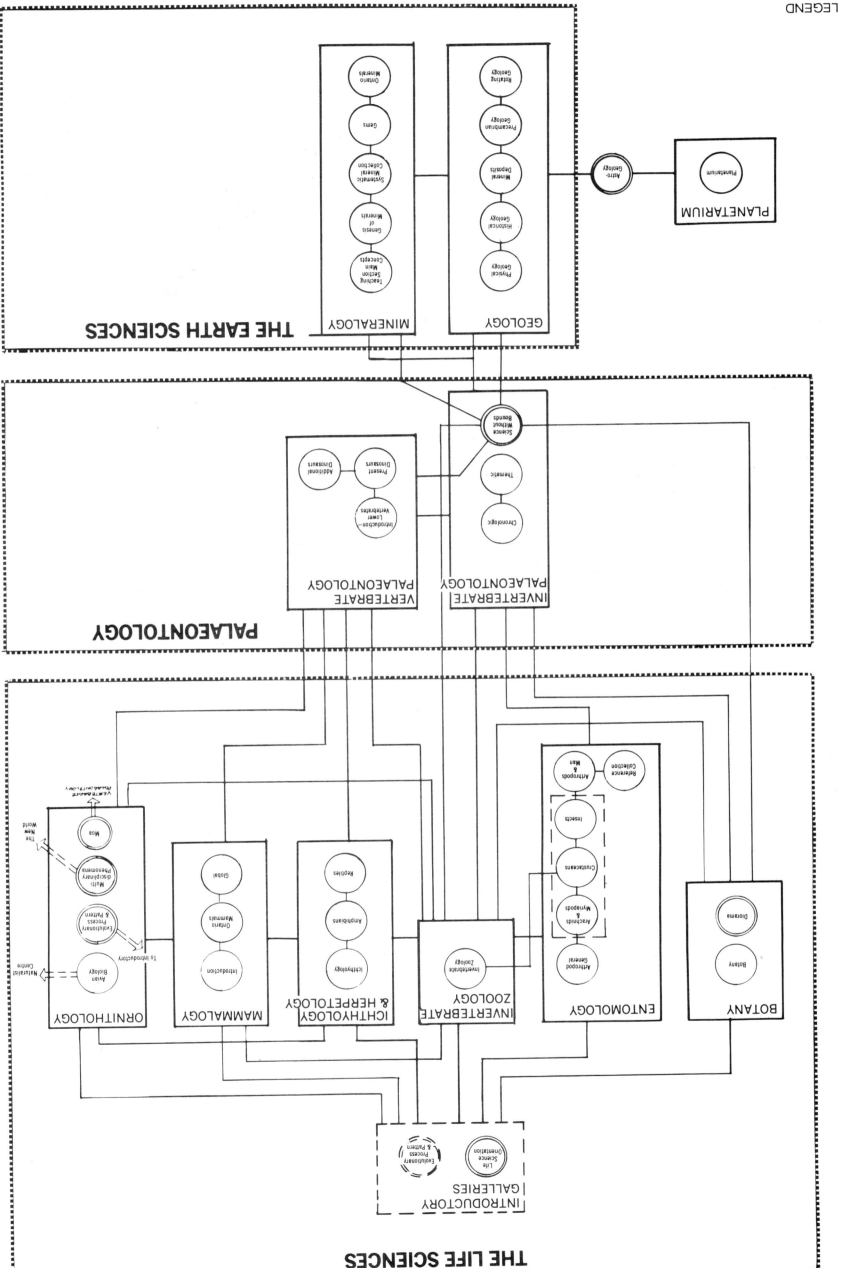

Figure 2: Interrelationship Diagram—Sciences

THE LIFE SCIENCES

INTRODUCTORY GALLERIES

Life Science Orientation

Evolutionary Process & Pattern

ORNITHOLOGY

Avian Biology · Evolutionary Process & Pattern · Multi-disciplinary Phenomena · Moa

To introductory
Naturalist Centre
The New World
VERTEBRATE PALAEONTOLOGY

MAMMALOGY

Introduction · Ontario Mammals · Global

ICHTHYOLOGY & HERPETOLOGY

Ichthyology · Amphibians · Reptiles

INVERTEBRATE ZOOLOGY

Invertebrate Zoology

ENTOMOLOGY

Arthropod General · Arachnids & Myriapods · Crustaceans · Insects · Arthropods & Man · Reference Collection

BOTANY

Botany · Diorama

PALAEONTOLOGY

VERTEBRATE PALAEONTOLOGY

Introduction · Lower Vertebrates · Present Dinosaurs · Additional Dinosaurs

INVERTEBRATE PALAEONTOLOGY

Chronologic · Thematic

Science Without Bounds

THE EARTH SCIENCES

MINERALOGY

Teaching Section Main Concepts · Genesis of Minerals · Systematic Mineral Collection · Gems · Ontario Minerals

GEOLOGY

Physical Geology · Historical Geology · Mineral Deposits · Precambrian Geology · Rotating Geology

Astro-Geology

PLANETARIUM

Planetarium

LEGEND

◎ Interdisciplinary gallery proposal

◯ Departmental gallery proposal

(◌) Interdisciplinary gallery – Suggested alternate relationship

⟜◯ Relationship exists with
◯⟜ Overlap of collections from

▭ Preliminary cluster suggestions
— Close conceptual relationship

Table V: Schedule of Gallery Development Activities 1978-1997

Years (each marked J A J O): 1978 1979 1980 1981 1982 1983 1984 1985 1986 1987 1988 1989 1990 1991 1992 1993 1994 1995 1996 1997

Legend:
- —— Gallery Development
- •••••••• Hold Construction for Access to Site
- —•—•— Evaluation and Modification

PHASE I

- Discovery Galleries (Level B2-Terrace)
- New World (Level B1-Terrace)
- Europe/Canada (Level B1-Terrace)
- Mankind Discovering (Level 1-Centre Block)
- Far East (Level 1-Terrace)
- Life Science Interdisciplinary (Level 2-Centre Block)
- Ancient World (Level 3-Terrace)
- Exhibition Hall (Level 1-SE Wing)

PHASE II

- Vertebrate Fossils (Level 2-NE Wing)
- Invertebrate Fossils (Level 2-SE Wing)
- Life Sciences (Level 3-East Wing)
- Ancient World (Level 2-Terrace)

PHASE III

- Earth Sciences (Level 1-SW Wing)
- Life Sciences Interdisciplinary (Level 2-Centre Block)
- Mammalogy (Level 2-SW Wing)
- Europe/Canada (Level 3-NE Wing)
- Ancient World (Level 3-W Wing and Centre Block)
- Invertebrate Galleries (Level 2-Terrace)
- New World (Level B1-Centre Block)
- Old World Ethnology (Level B1-Centre Block)
- Herpetology (Level 2-SE Wing)
- Ornithology (Level 2-SE Wing)
- Botany (Level 2-NW Wing)
- Ichthyology (Level 2-NW Wing)
- Mammalogy (Level 2-NW Wing)
- Far East (Level 1-NW Wing)
- Europe/Canada (Level 3-SE Wing)
- Planetarium (Planetarium)
- Vertebrate Fossils (Level 2-NE Wing)

Figure 28: European Cluster

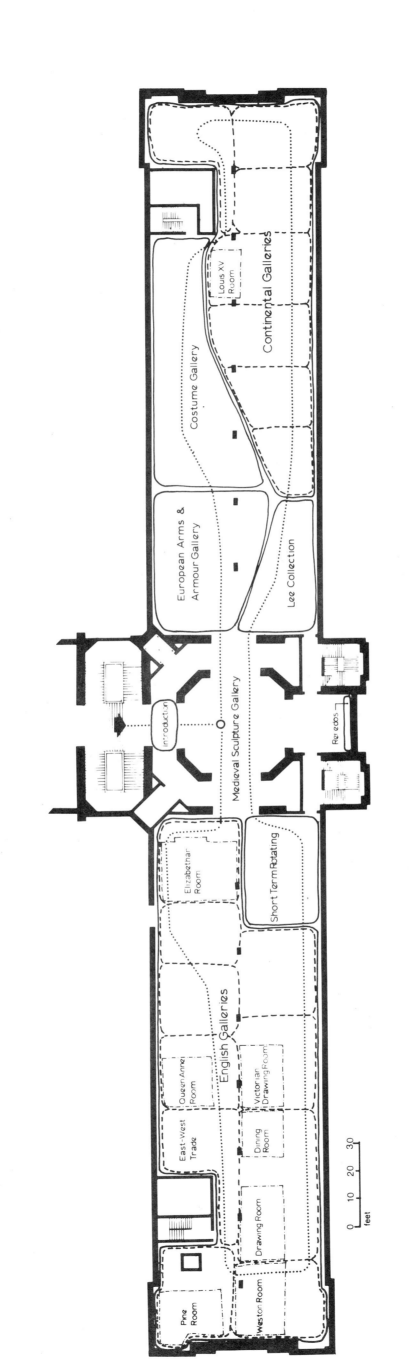

Pine Room

Weston Room

Drawing Room

East-West Trade

Queen Anne Room

Dining Room

Victorian Drawing Room

English Galleries

Elizabethan Room

Short Term Rotating

Introduction

Medieval Sculpture Gallery

Reredos

European Arms & Armour Gallery

Lee Collection

Costume Gallery

Louis XV Room

Continental Galleries

0 10 20 30

feet

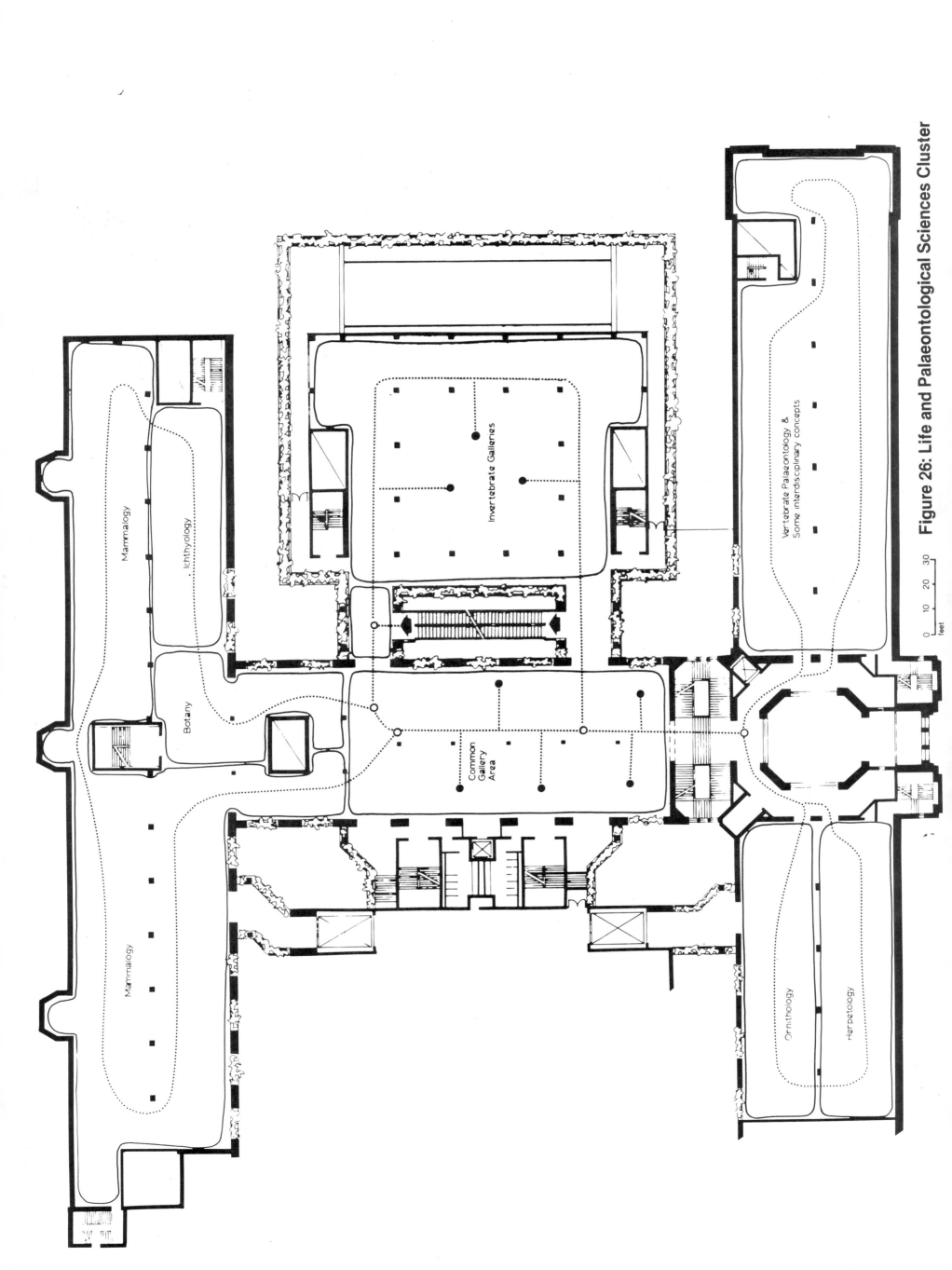

Figure 26: Life and Palaeontological Sciences Cluster

Mammalogy

Ichthyology

Mammalogy

Botany

Common Gallery Area

Invertebrate Galleries

Vertebrate Palaeontology & Some interdisciplinary concepts

Ornithology

Herpetology

0   10   20   30
feet